CUBA

THE PEARL OF THE CARIBBEAN

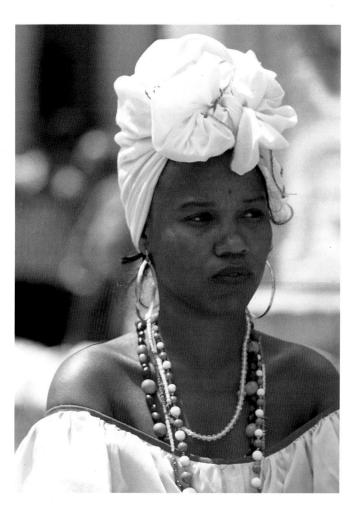

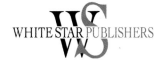

WHITE STAR PUBLISHERS

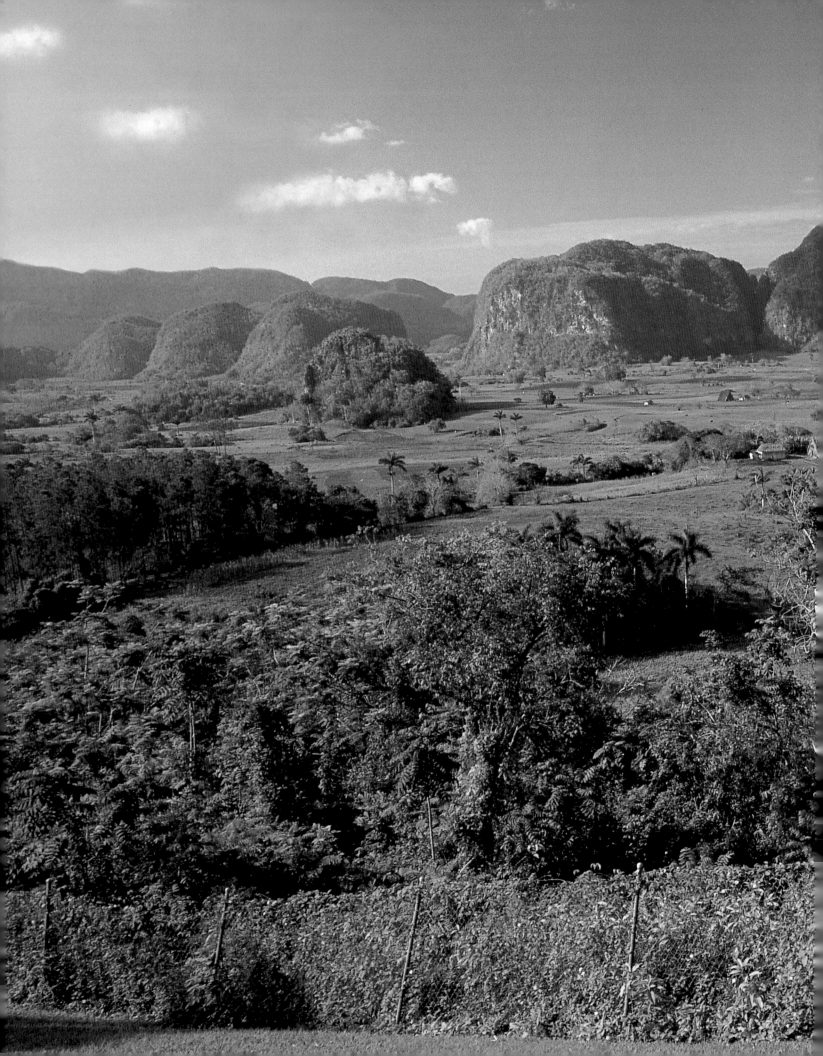

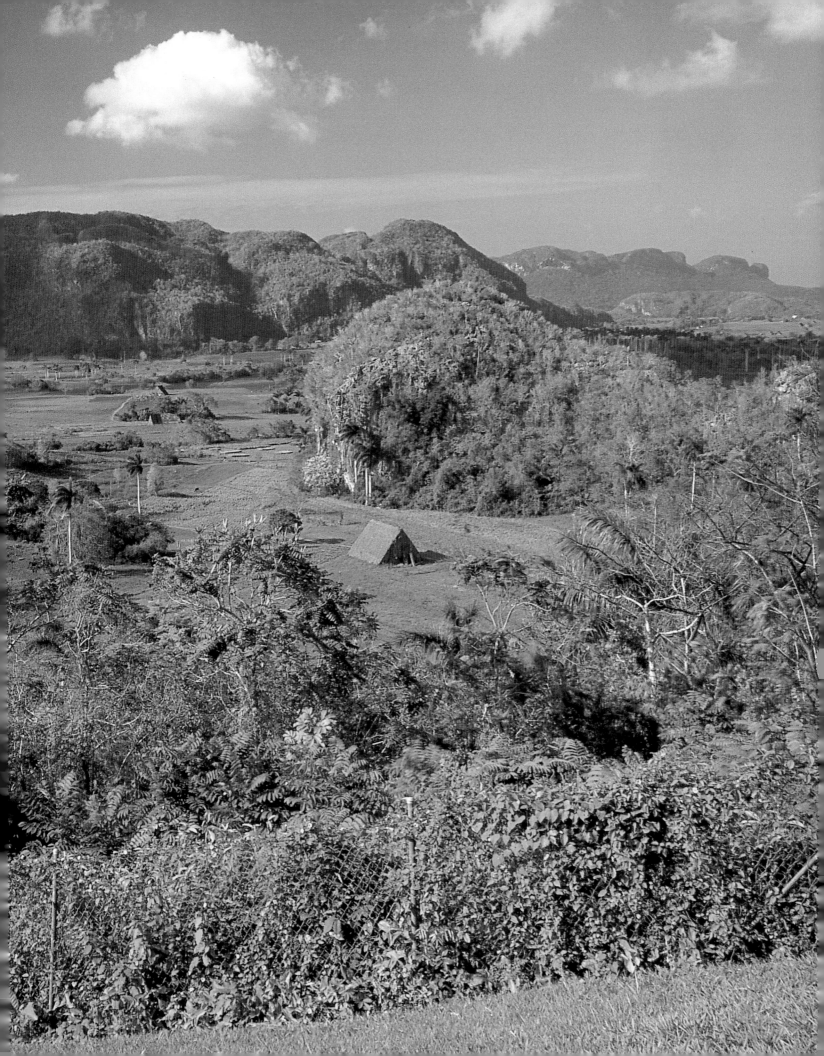

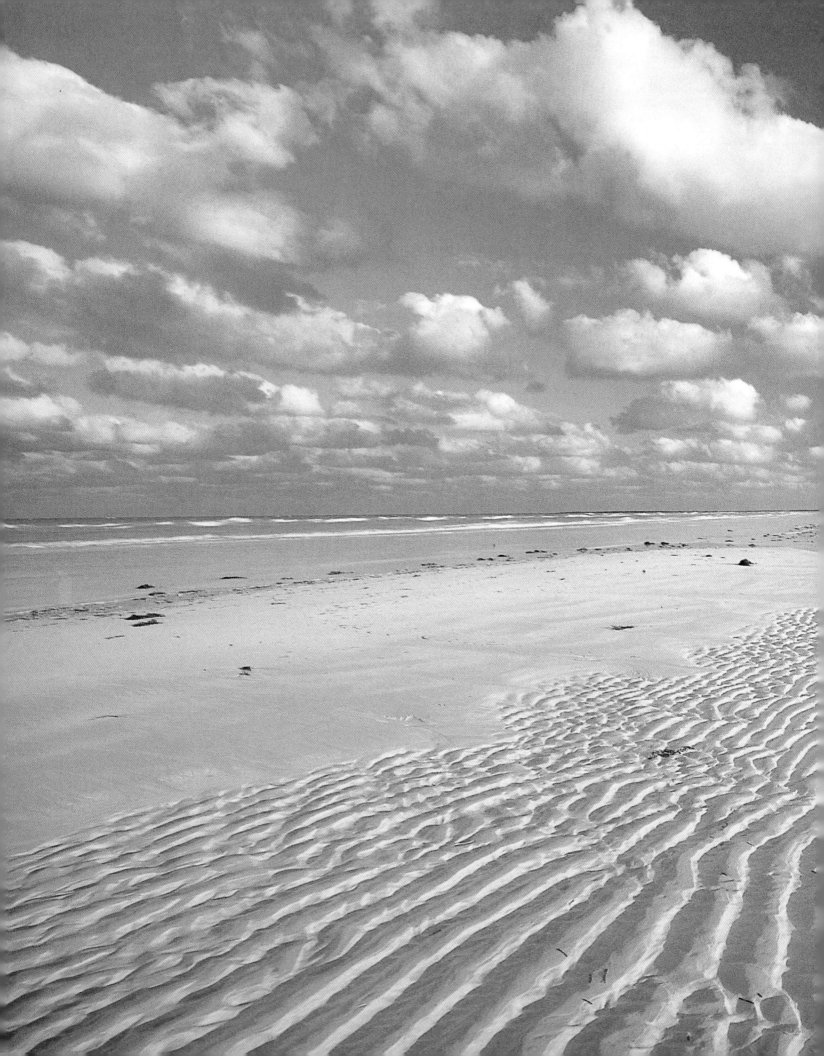

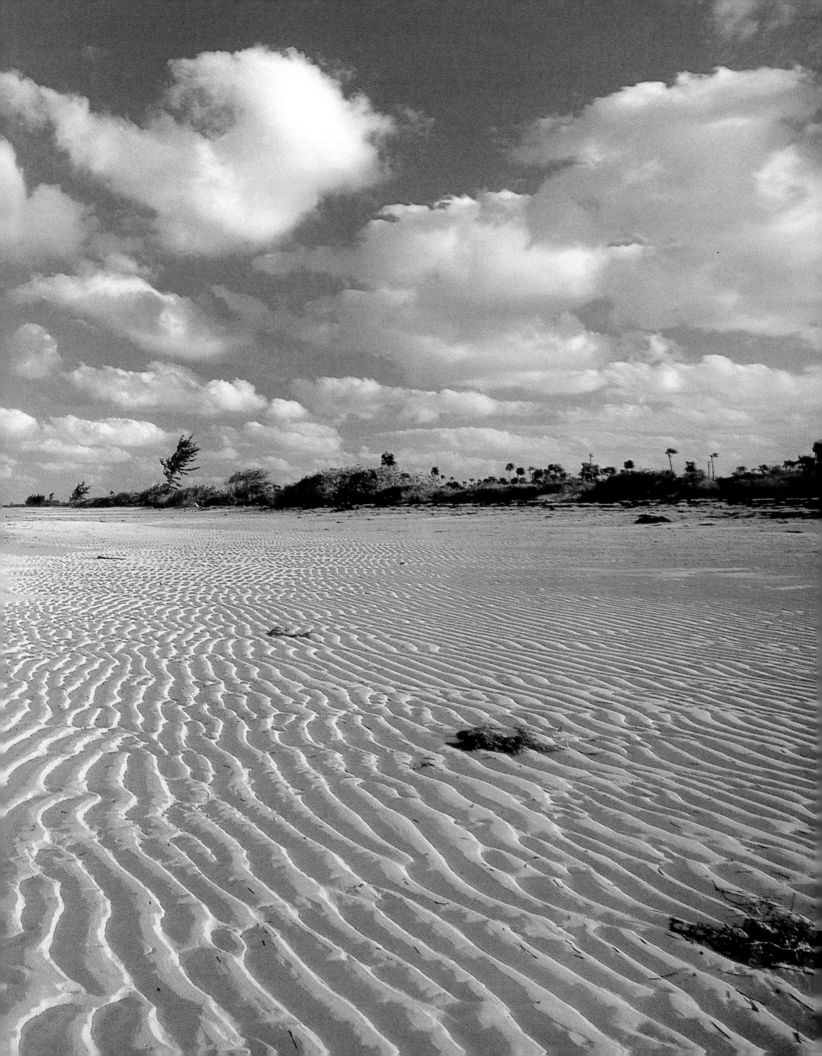

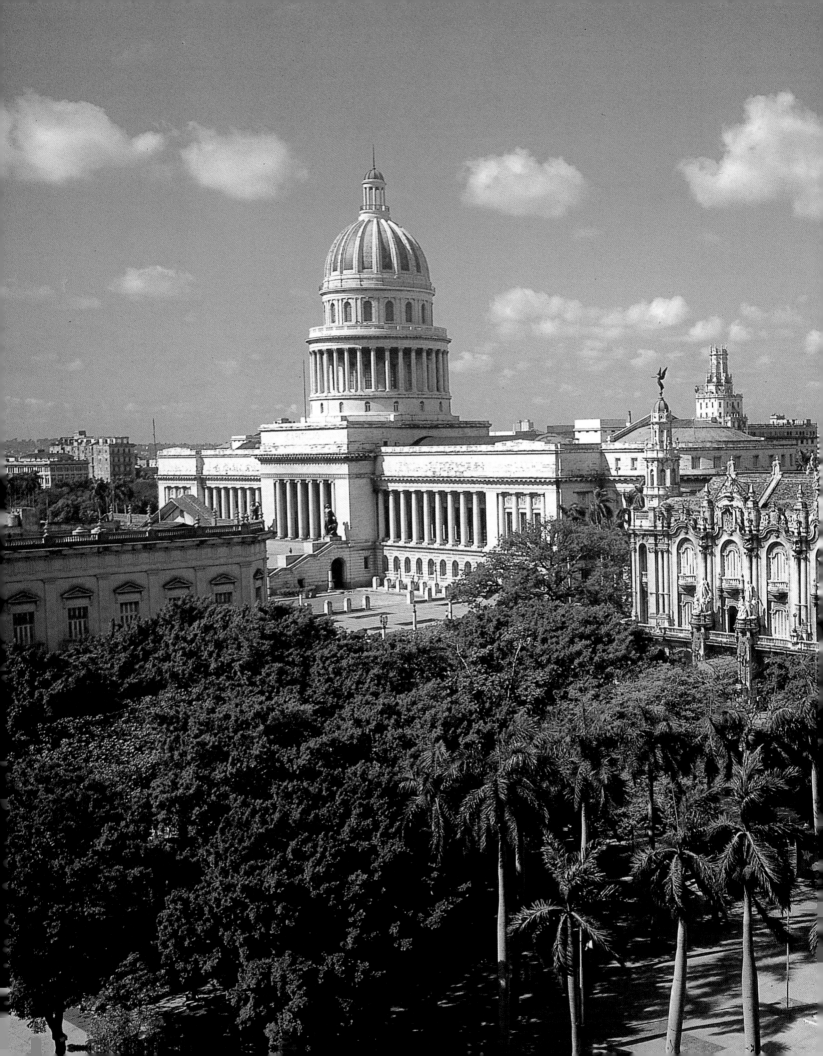

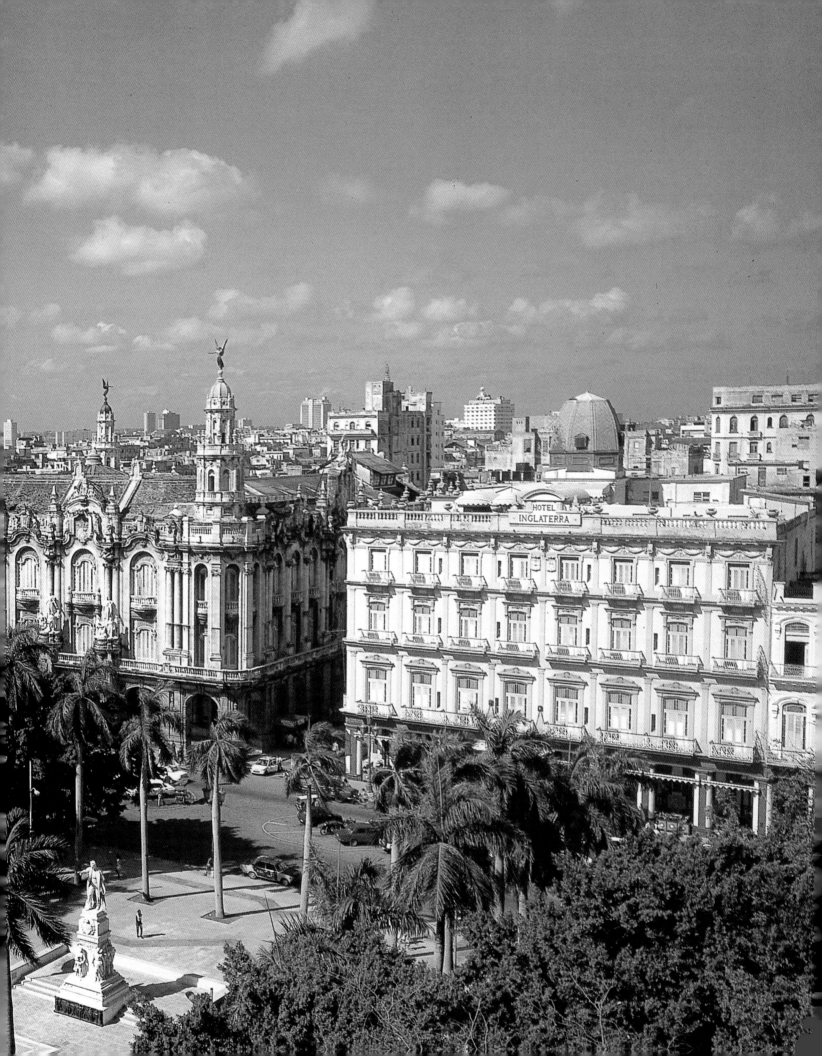

Text
Paolo Rinaldi

Graphic design
Anna Galliani

Translation
Ann Ghiringhelli

Photographs
Antonio Attini

Contents

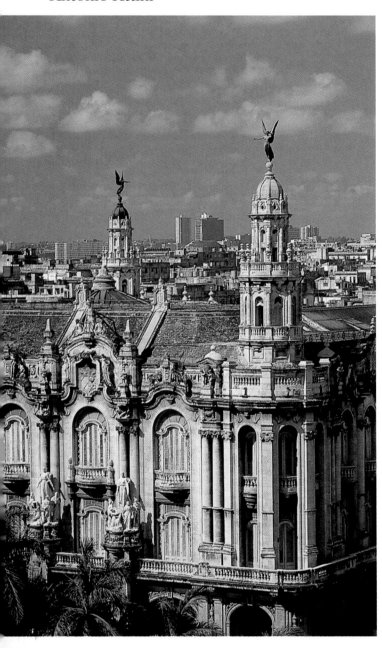

1 *The women of Cuba have always been renowned for their beauty, their smooth amber skin, silky hair and seductive smile. Some of the loveliest can be seen performing in floor-shows at the Tropicana,* Havana's celebrated nightclub.

2-3 *Located in the Sierra de los Organos, west of Havana, in Pinar del Río province, is the valley of Viñales. Its geological origin is of exceptional interest: the valley was once a vast cavern-like formation that stretched across several thousand acres; it had hills – called mogotes – that, like gigantic pillars, supported a ceiling, which later crumbled away. What remains – the valley of Viñales – is a magical place.*

4-5 *Playa Paredòn is one of the finest beaches on Cayo Coco, the largest of the islands that form an archipelago, of 52 square miles, off the coast of Ciego de Avila. All of them are uninhabited and unspoilt. The only exceptions are Cayo Coco and Cayo Guillermo, where tourist structures have now been built. But their impact on the natural environment is closely monitored by scientists from Havana University.*

6-7 *In Havana, overlooking the open Parque Central with its statue of José Martí, are several 18th-century buildings, including the Hotel Inglaterra. Rising up behind them is the dome of the Capitolio Nacional.*

8 *The Gran Teatro is an eye-catching structure, built in an eclectic style with touches of both Gothic and Renaissance, and contains several auditoria, including the García Lorca Hall. Locals often refer to the whole theater as the "García Lorca". It is the home of the Cuban National Ballet.*

9 *Among the natural wonders of the valley of Viñales are the picturesque waterfall at Soroa, in the western part of Pinar del Río; the Cueva del Indio, a cavern through which an underground stream flows; the Cueva di San Miguel; and the Paredòn del Eco, where visitors who climb the hillside are rewarded with the sound of their echoing voices. A drawing on the rock face called Mural de la Prehistoria is in fact a modern representation of the history of the world.*

© 1999, 2007 White Star S.p.A.
Via C. Sassone, 22/24
13100 Vercelli, Italy
www.whitestar.it

New updated edition

ISBN 978-88-544-0362-8

Reprints:
1 2 3 4 5 6   11 10 09 08 07

Color separations by Fotomec, Turin and Bassoli, Milan

Printed in Singapore

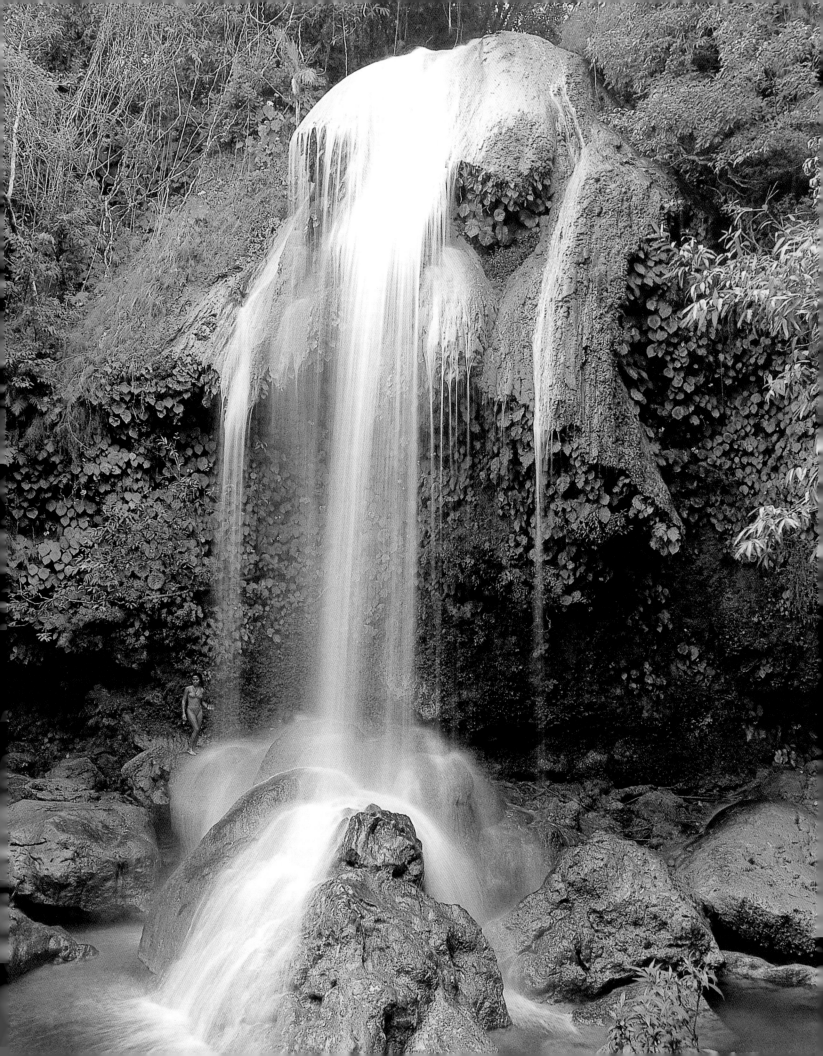

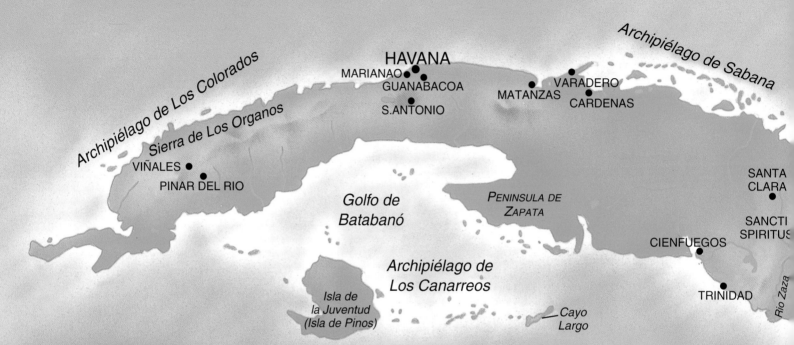

GULF
OF MEXICO

Florida Keys

Archipiélago de Los Colorados

Sierra de Los Organos

HAVANA

MARIANAO
GUANABACOA
S.ANTONIO

Archipiélago de Sabana

VARADERO
MATANZAS
CARDENAS

VIÑALES
PINAR DEL RIO

Golfo de
Batabanó

PENINSULA DE
ZAPATA

SANTA
CLARA

SANCTI
SPIRITUS

CIENFUEGOS

Archipiélago de
Los Canarreos

TRINIDAD

Rio Zaza

Isla de
la Juventud
(Isla de Pinos)

Cayo
Largo

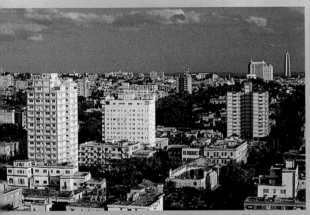

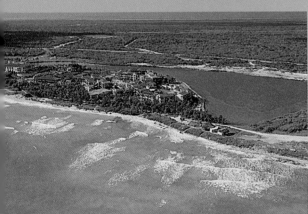

10 top *Seen here from the air is the Vedado district of Havana, dotted with skyscrapers. The city, with its two million inhabitants, radiates outwards from the bay; it covers a vast area but sites of tourist interest are concentrated in the center. The urban core consists of three districts: Vedado, Old Havana and Central Havana, which together extend – east-west – for 4 miles*

10 bottom *An aerial view of the tourist village of Cayo Coco, built on the island of the same name and linked by road, across a causeway, with the little town of Moron, on the coast of Ciego de Avila province. Strict controls are now in place to protect the extremely complex and delicate natural environment of the cays.*

11 top *Trinidad, in the Sancti Spiritus region, was founded by the Spanish in 1514. In the 18th century it was an important trading center for tobacco and sugarcane. It was later abandoned and remained cut off from the rest of the world until 1920 when the railway line to Placetas was inaugurated. Restoration of the town's colonial buildings began in 1967 and it became a designated UNESCO World Heritage Site in 1988.*

11 bottom *The Sierra del Escambray, between Cienfuegos and Trinidad, is a rugged mountainous region characterized by high peaks and steep slopes; communications have always been difficult in this area, which has not infrequently provided safe hideaways for armed guerrilla groups.*

Cayman
Islands

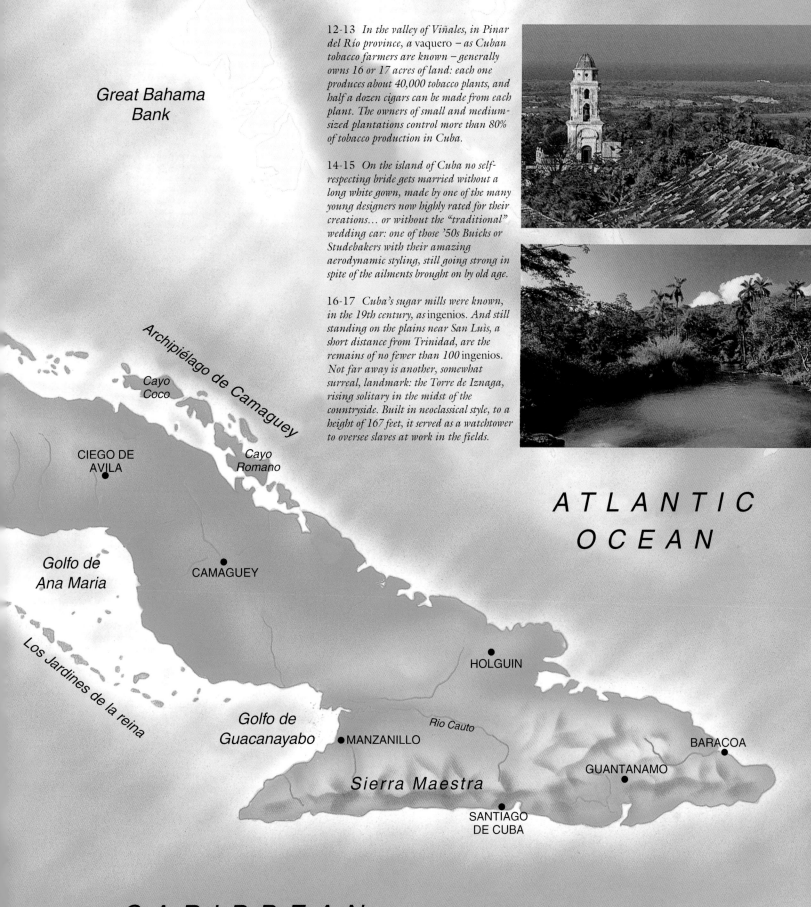

12-13 In the valley of Viñales, in Pinar del Río province, a vaquero – as Cuban tobacco farmers are known – generally owns 16 or 17 acres of land: each one produces about 40,000 tobacco plants, and half a dozen cigars can be made from each plant. The owners of small and medium-sized plantations control more than 80% of tobacco production in Cuba.

14-15 On the island of Cuba no self-respecting bride gets married without a long white gown, made by one of the many young designers now highly rated for their creations… or without the "traditional" wedding car: one of those '50s Buicks or Studebakers with their amazing aerodynamic styling, still going strong in spite of the ailments brought on by old age.

16-17 Cuba's sugar mills were known, in the 19th century, as ingenios. And still standing on the plains near San Luìs, a short distance from Trinidad, are the remains of no fewer than 100 ingenios. Not far away is another, somewhat surreal, landmark: the Torre de Iznaga, rising solitary in the midst of the countryside. Built in neoclassical style, to a height of 167 feet, it served as a watchtower to oversee slaves at work in the fields.

Great Bahama
Bank

Archipiélago de Camaguey

Cayo
Coco

Cayo
Romano

CIEGO DE
AVILA

ATLANTIC
OCEAN

Golfo de
Ana Maria

CAMAGUEY

Los Jardines de la reina

HOLGUIN

Golfo de
Guacanayabo

Rio Cauto

MANZANILLO

BARACOA

GUANTANAMO

Sierra Maestra

SANTIAGO
DE CUBA

CARIBBEAN
SEA

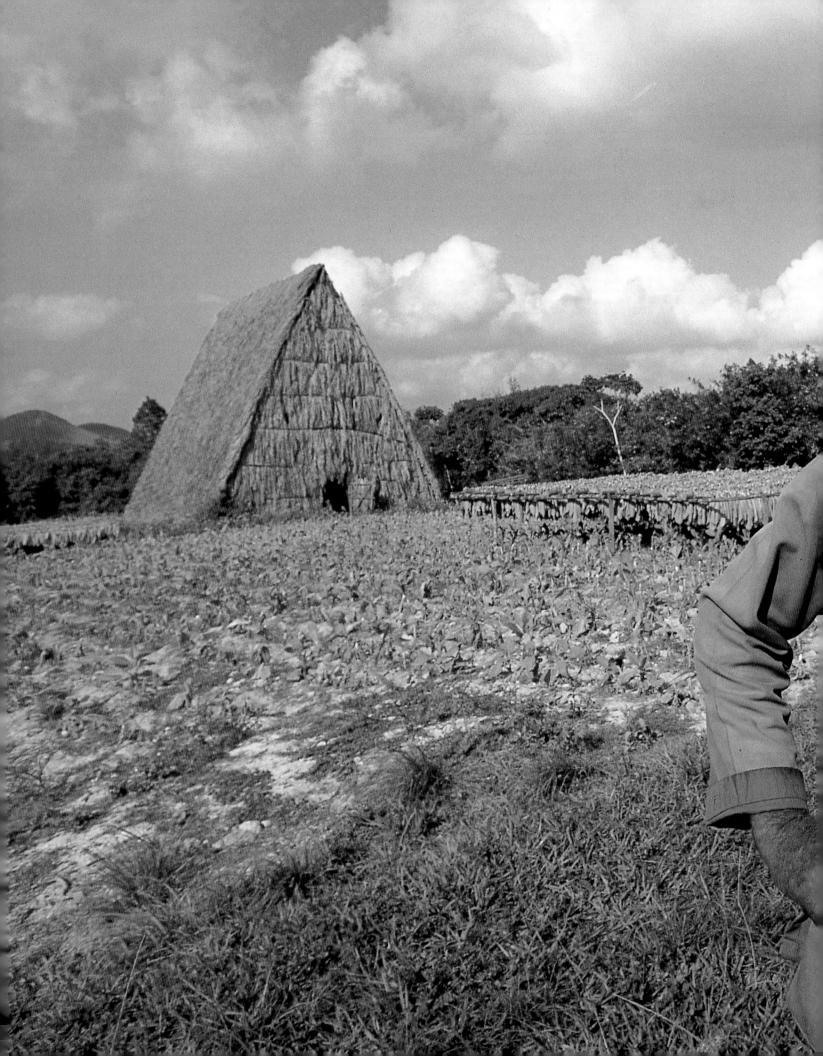

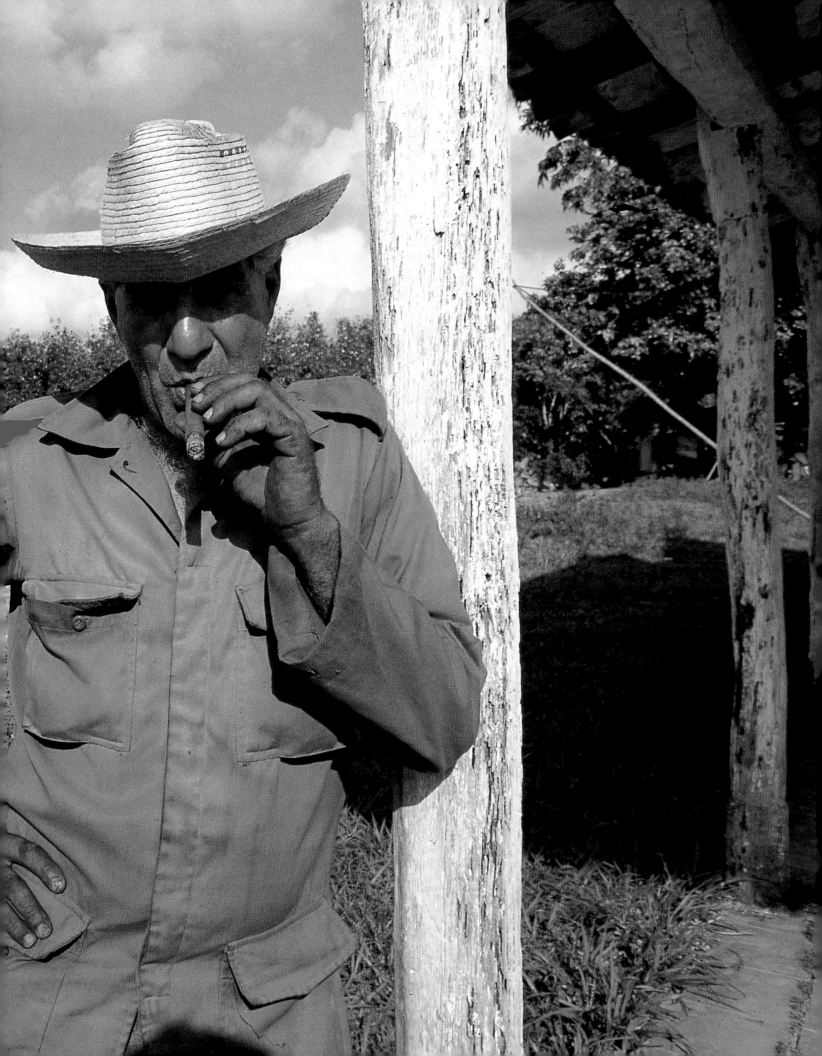

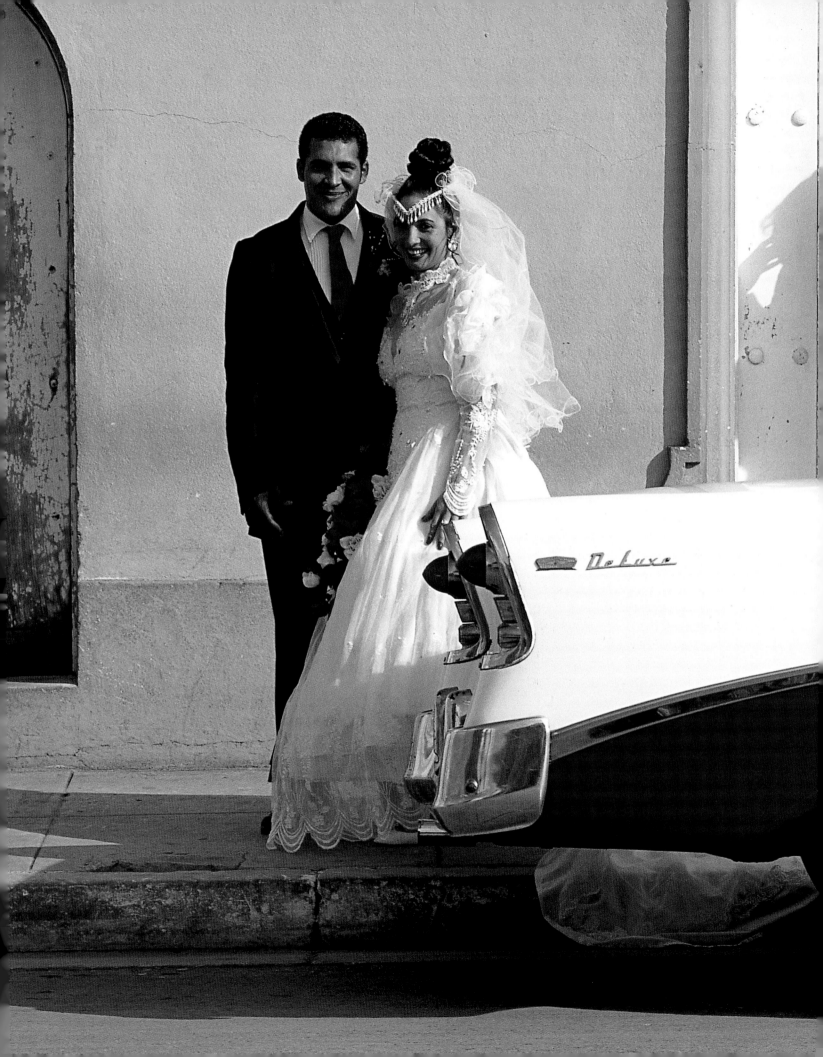

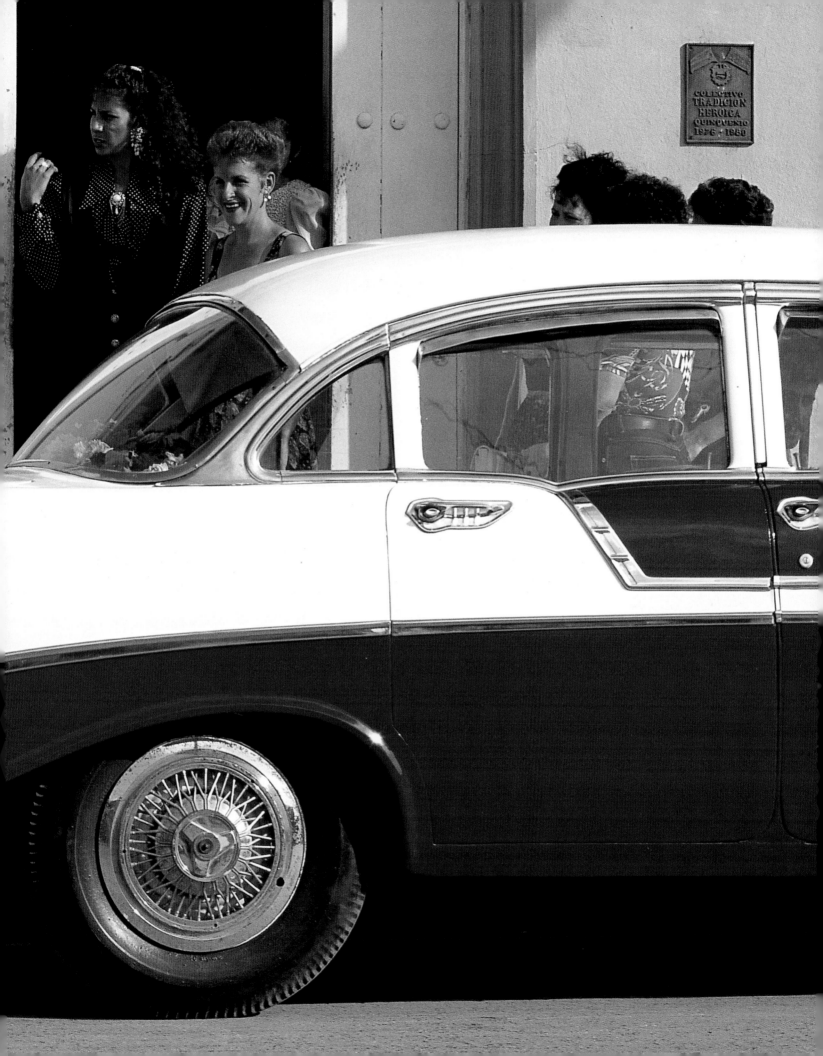

Introduction

Five hundred years have passed since Christopher Columbus caught sight of the shores of Cuba and said he had never seen a place more beautiful. Still today, disembarking travellers are almost overwhelmed by the light, colors and pulsating rhythms of this enchanting and friendly land.

The island of Cuba, set in the Caribbean Sea, is 746 miles long, the largest of the many islands that fringe the Gulf of Mexico. Ringing it are five archipelagoes – Camaguey is the second largest in the world – formed by over 4,000 coral cays. Almost all of them are uninhabited and still untamed, with the exception of two off the southern shores: Cayo Largo and Isla de la Juventud (the largest of the islands around Cuba, also known as Isla de Pinos), in the Archipélago de los Canarreos. Thanks to their deserted beaches and sea floors thick with coral, including rare black coral, these islands are now immensely popular destinations for international tourists, frequented by divers, sailing enthusiasts and vacationers in search of life's simple pleasures.

The cays (or keys) dotted along both Caribbean and Atlantic coasts of Cuba are geologically young and classified as barrier-islands: some are formed of deposited sand of coral and rock origin; others originate from mangroves that sink their roots into the muddy bed and, aided by the wind, create new stretches of land. In this case they are described as "islands in movement", best explored with catamarans that can be manoeuvred through the shallow waters. The interior of the island is intensely green, its natural landscape having changed little since the days of the earliest colonists. Areas not cultivated with sugar plantations are covered by forests, hills where tobacco is grown and the mountains of the Sierra. Vast tracts are now sanctuaries for threatened animal species or wildlife species. As well as these national parks, Cuba has four biosphere reserves, established under the aegis of UNESCO.

When Christopher Columbus landed here, Cuba was home to Guanahatabey, Siboney and Taino Indians. Within the space of a few decades the native population was decimated: only 5,000 were left of the 100,000 Indians who inhabited Cuba at the time of the conquest. The colonial period lasted almost four centuries, from 1510 to 1902 when, at the end of a struggle that had started in 1868, Cuba declared its independence from Spain and became a republic. The conquest of the island had been led by Diego Velázquez, who also founded the island's main settlements. In 1517 twelve black slaves arrived here – the first of tens of thousands who eventually became the core of the Cuban nation. With its stunning natural harbor, Havana quickly became the sorting house for the treasures plundered by the Spanish, as well a hotbed of international piracy. The present Isla de la Juventud provided an ideal haven for buccaneers and pirates between raids. It was at this time that the city of Havana was fortified.

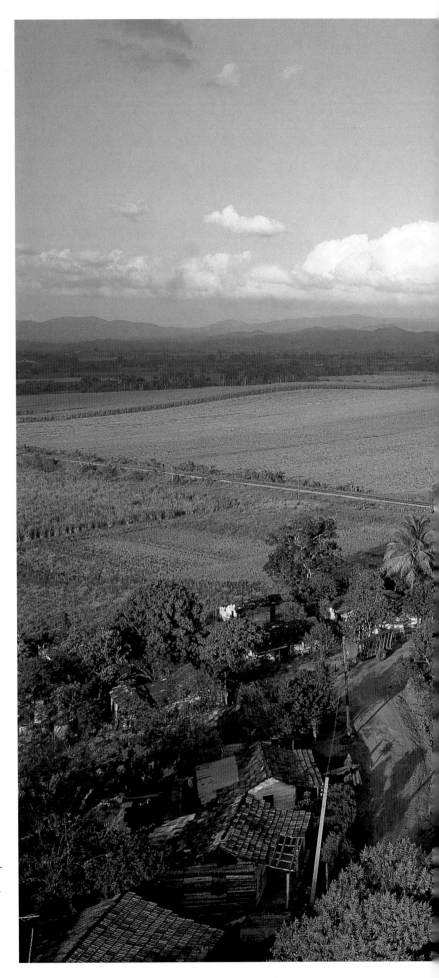

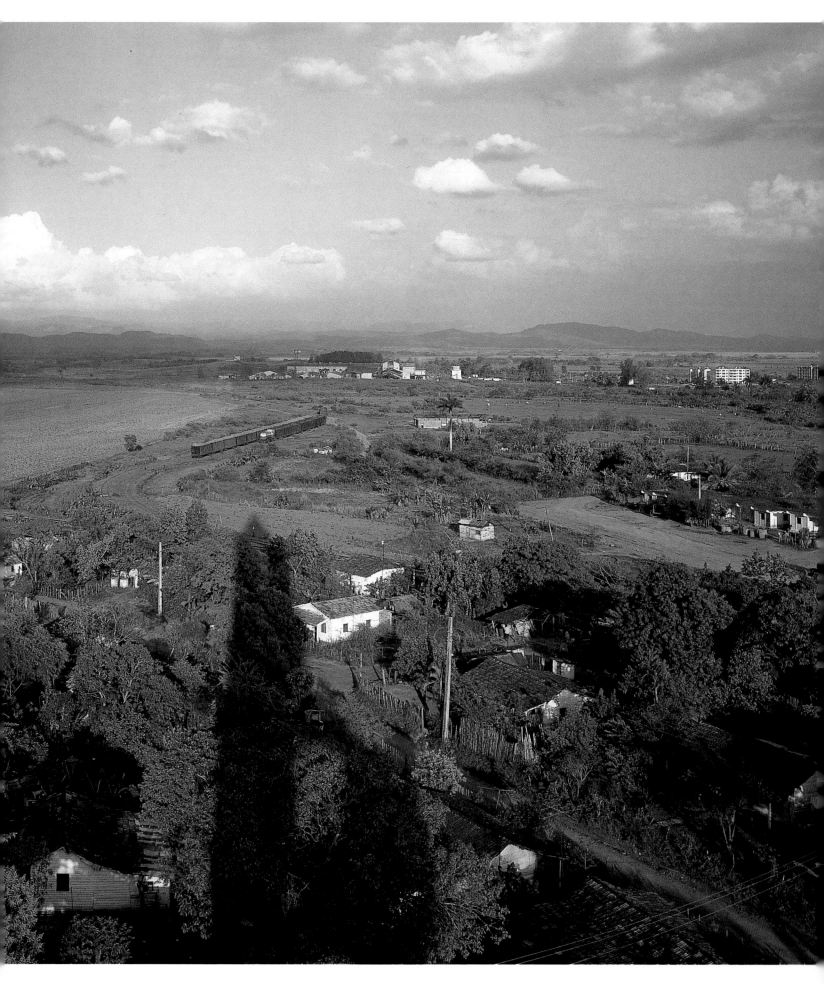

By 1600 Cuba was surrounded by hostile islands and territories: Jamaica, Guyana and Barbados had been settled by the British; Tortuga, Guadaloupe and Martinique were in French hands; the Virgin Islands and Guyana were controlled by the Dutch. In 1697 the Treaty of Ryswick brought piracy to an end. In Cuba this same century had also seen the spread of sugar and tobacco plantations, a fast population growth, among both blacks and whites, and the total extinction of the native Indians. The creoles appeared on the scene – children of Spaniards, born on the island. The people of Cuba thus began to form a single nation, integrated in the few schools, run by priests or nuns. Their religious beliefs, icons and rites merged into a colorful syncretism, eventually – in the 20th century – forced into hibernation by Castro's regime, but now making a strong comeback.

From the 18th century to the Revolution Cuba's history was interspersed with uprisings, guerrilla warfare and outbursts of political fervor, during rule first by the Spanish, then by the British and, in 1763, by the Spanish again. In a short space of time a series of fortuitous events turned the island into the world's leading sugar producer. In the early 19th century came the start, in Latin America, of wars of independence fought to obtain political autonomy from Spain, but Cuba was not actively involved. Around 1850 the island was shaken by a series of uprisings aimed at liberating Cuba from Spanish rule; all of them came to nothing. The first war of independence erupted in 1868 and lasted 10 years. Slavery was abolished in 1886. War broke out again in 1895. After an explosion on board the US cruiser "Maine", in 1898 the Americans took over control of the island from Spain and began to make their economic influence felt there. The following years were marked by a succession of dictators and puppet-presidents, until a young lawyer named Fidel Castro appeared on the scene. A great destiny awaited him. On July 26th 1953 he led a group of revolutionaries against the Moncada military barracks. The attack failed; Castro was captured, tried and condemned to exile in Mexico. There he eventually joined forces with the group led by Ernesto "Che" Guevara. Castro returned to Cuba at the end of 1956, aboard the "Granma", and in 1957 retreated into the mountains of the Sierra Maestra to wage the guerrilla warfare that eventually led him to victory.

After fifty years of struggles and profound political and social conflict, in 1959 the revolution and the formation of the government headed by Fidel Castro marked the start of an era of social and cultural change. With the new regime came solutions to major problems like housing, employment, education and health care. Regrettably all these conquests were partly nullified, years later, by the fall of the Soviet empire, which had become Cuba's main economic partner after the *bloqueo*, the economic embargo imposed by the US since 1990. Abandoned by Russia and isolated by the *bloqueo*, Cuba has been through a period so critical it seemed to be at death's door. In their state of proud isolation, Cubans have been severely tested by the so-called *periodo especial*: transport services halved, intermittent electricity supply, empty shelves in the shops, factories closed, hospitals without medicines. Today the worst is over and things are looking up. The signs of recovery are many and can be spotted in the countryside as

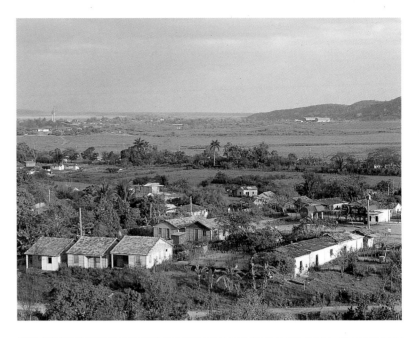

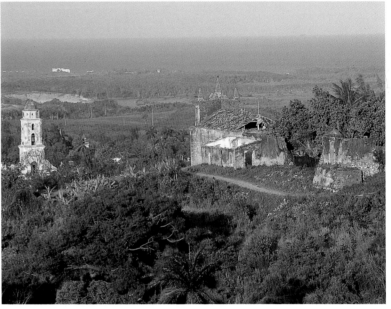

18 top *The Valley Los Ingenios was once the site of mills where cane was crushed to extract its juice and produce sugar. It is now dotted with small villages, clustered around San Lùis. The valley extends at the foot of the Sierra del Escambray: nowadays this impervious and almost impenetrable region – refuge of guerrilla groups in the years of the Castrist Revolution – is inhabited by isolated families that live in* bohìos, *thatched huts perched on the slopes of the mountains.*

18 bottom *Trinidad is perched on a hill overlooking the sea but in the 18th century its position did not save it from attacks by the pirates who roamed the Caribbean. After the town had been*

plundered several times, its people decided to pay a corsair to defend them. Before long, however, they became pirates themselves and, in the history of buccaneering, enjoyed their own short period of notoriety. Thanks to these forays, Trinidad became a very wealthy city.

19 *Farming in the valley of Viñales has not yet been mechanized. Peasants still use traditional ploughs drawn by oxen, and sow seed by hand. In the region of Pinar del Río, tobacco plantations cover more than 98,840 hectares, corresponding to 3,000* caballerìas *(this unit of measurement, formerly in use in Cuba, was calculated by the distance a horse could travel in a set time).*

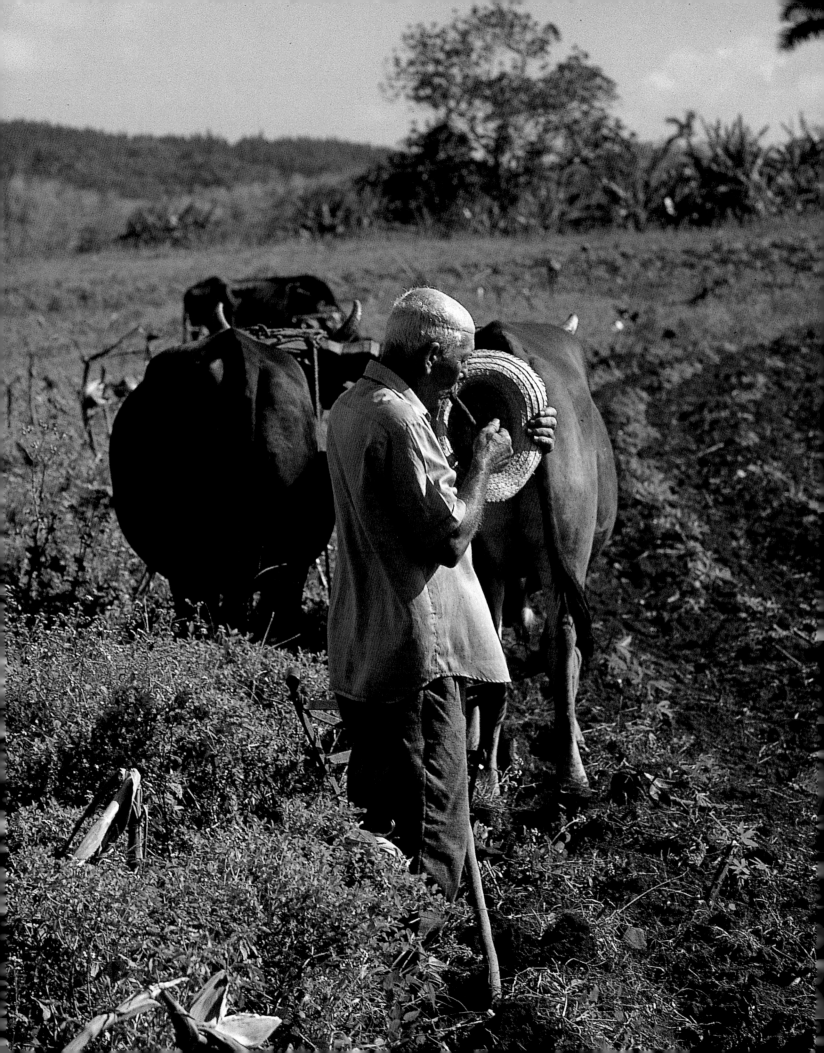

well as in the capital and other major cities. The filming lights are also those of the *paladares*: since the Cuban Tourism Ministry gave restaurant licenses to private individuals, thousands of small bistros named after a soap opera set in a little family restaurant called "Paladar" have sprung up. On green patios perfumed with hibiscus, typical dishes, both simple and delicious, are prepared. They are nectar for tourists, who find fragments from another Cuba in these little joints, far from stereotypes and the "all-included" packages offered by tour operators. The *paladares* have popped up in practically every neighborhood, and they can be recognized by their funny names and lively signs in addition to the ever-present hawkers promoting them. They are also fairly difficult to find – you have to ask the locals – since they may be "here one day, gone the next." But they've become an excellent opportunity to taste real Cuban food. The island's cuisine stems from its mix of African and Spanish cultures, with French influence in the Baracoa region too. The Spanish contributed mainly rice, citrus fruit, pork and beef; from Africa came yam, the potato-like taro, and bananas; on the island the settlers found corn, manioc and sweet potatoes. These same typically *criolla* dishes are still served in Cuba today. Rice is the staple, together with black beans, used for a dish called *Moros y Cristianos* or for *congrì*: rice, beans and small pieces of bacon fat. Plus, of course, Chinese-style fried rice (in the 19th century large number of Chinese laborers were brought to the island by the Spanish, as cheap labor). Other popular Cuban specialities are pork and chicken cooked in the creole fashion… as well as *enchiladas* (stews), lobster and countless recipes using fish. There is an amazing assortment of desserts on offer: for instance, *malarrabia*, made from orange peel, cane syrup and cinnamon; *natilla*, a delicious cream; and wonderful ice-creams. Exquisite desserts are prepared from all the fruit found on the island: guava peel, candied coconut, papaya, pineapple and orange.

No description of Cuba would be complete without a special mention of rum, described by Cuban writer Fernandez Campoamor as sugarcane's "happy-go-lucky child". Rum – the Cubans call it *ron* – tastes good drunk neat or as a base for original and superb cocktails: mojito (rum, mint leaves, sugar, soda and lime), daiquiri (crushed ice, rum, sugar and lime), Cuba Libre, Ron Collins, Mary Pickford and many more. Back in the 16th century rum was the favorite drink of buccaneers and pirates. At that time it was a hellish, bitter-tasting liquid, known in fact as 'kill-devil'. Nowadays it is a fine-quality, aromatic product obtained from a long and sophisticated process to distil *aguardiente* from the fermented juice of sugarcane. There are three main types: *carta blanca* (from the color of the label) three years old, dry and light, ideal for cocktails; *carta oro*, five years old, dry and golden in color, for drinking neat; *anejo*, at least seven years old, full-bodied and mellow.

All over the island people continue to drink rum and smoke *puros* but at mealtimes the fare is often meagre. A popular place to eat is in the food markets run by peasants in every town and village. The finest is Cuatro Caminos, in the center of Havana. Here you can buy *cajitas*, cardboard boxes containing a mini-meal that cost about one dollar apiece. It is in places like this that the true atmosphere of Cuba can be savored, as in cafés and taverns that may have

20 top *Not only tobacco is grown in the valley of Viñales. This photo shows a peasant carrying two clusters of bananas, grown in one of the many banana groves that flourish in the region. The valley has no sugarcane plantations, which have displaced practically every other crop elsewhere on the island.*

20 bottom *In 18th-century Cuba no self-respecting estate was without its long line of royal palms, trees of exceptional elegance thanks to their smooth trunks and great height. There are still rows of these trees on the island today: the ones in this picture form the backdrop to a field – ploughed the traditional way – in the valley of Viñales, in Pinar del Río province.*

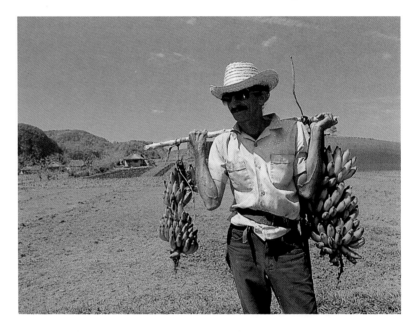

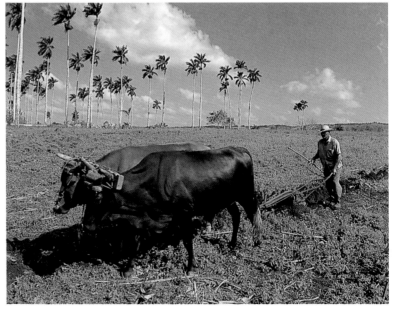

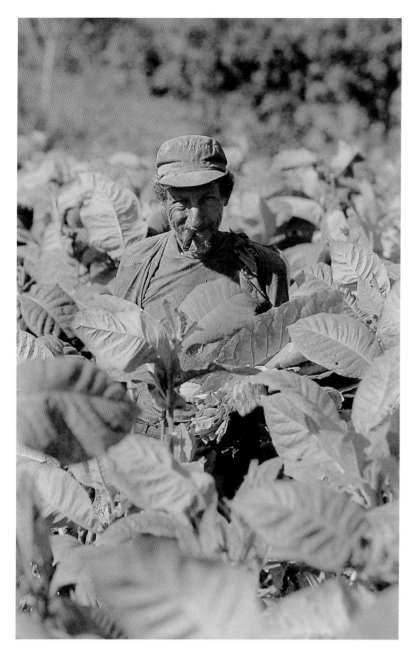

21 *A tobacco farmer on a plantation in the valley of Viñales. The plants, practically as tall as the man himself, have about 20 leaves each. From a distance they look like rows of soldiers, each dark green strip seemingly ready to attack the surrounding hillsides on which age-old cedar trees grow. The wood of these same cedars is used to make the cigar boxes whose labels are much sought-after by collectors.*

the forlorn look of rundown country houses: food and drink are nearly always in short supply but there's bound to be music (even if played on primitive, "homemade" instruments like tin drums). In Cuba every occasion is an excuse for music and song. If bars and clubs are shut, then people make music in their homes or in the streets. Music pervades Cuban life, with rhythms that add African beats to Spanish melodies, producing son, salsa, cha-cha-cha, danzòn, rumba, guaracha, bolero and mambo. As dark descends on Havana the whole city comes to life, swinging and swaying through the night, and in clubs and bars tireless revellers dance on until dawn. No crisis can silence the island's music, stop its pulsating rhythms or stifle the Cubans' infinite enthusiasm for life. As elsewhere, the younger generation now prefers rock to traditional and folk music and there are numerous groups playing seriously heavy "heavy metal". Jazz has received the stamp of official approval, and Cuban bands often tour abroad. No longer considered an imperialist sign of American capitalism, jazz is played in the Karl Marx theater, and in government-sponsored cultural centers across the island. Ballet has an important tradition in Cuba and it produced an outstanding ballerina, Alicia Alonso, now a revered teacher.

The ability of Cubans to face the problems of daily life has been put to the test over the years of economic crisis. The initiatives of individuals have contributed more and more to the available public facilities as impromptu means of transportation demonstrate, usually entrusted to buses called *guagua* but often flanked by totally original private vehicles such as the *cyclo-pousse*, rickshaw-bicycles, camels, and couriers made out of ex-train cars. Even the ways of accommodating tourists has changed over recent years: private individuals have been allowed to open their homes to paying guests who, just like in the *paladares*, can sample Cuban hospitality at a convenient price. Lodging in a private home starts at 15 dollars per night, but it is not actually rent: it is rather a contribution to expenses, maintenance, and upkeep.

The historic centers of the most important cities – Baracoa, Bayamo, Trinidad, Santiago de Cuba and Havana – have survived practically intact; the "old towns" of Trinidad and Havana are designated UNESCO World Heritage sites. In spite of its economic trials and tribulations, the government has not neglected the island's architectural assets: colonial buildings and monuments have been restored, historic sites conserved and numerous museums established. Cuba's capital, founded by the Spanish in 1519, has acquired almost legendary status. Far from being provincial, Havana is a modern and cosmopolitan city, currently re-assuming the splendor of its past. The passing centuries have had little impact on the original colonial layout and many of its old urban and architectural features have survived. In Old Havana three squares are distinguished by their respective functions: religious in Plaza de la Catedral, political and military in Plaza de Armas and commercial in Plaza Vieja. Every period of colonial architecture is richly represented in Havana, from testimonies left by the very earliest settlers to the climax of baroque. Yet no changes have marred the city's distinctive traditional features: shady patios, kaleidoscopic effects of light and color, arched colonnades, minimal furnishings. Eusepio Leal, Historiador de la

Ciudad, described Havana as "one of the most incredible examples of architectural eclecticism ever produced, a city in which the encounter of late baroque and the Italian Renaissance result in what seems like a huge magical plaything". Fidel Castro put this historian in charge of giving a face-lift to the old nucleus of the city, with funds firstly provided by UNESCO and later begged or borrowed from foundations, foreign communities and industrialists. Many monuments and historic buildings have been restored and handsome old structures converted into museums, hotels and cafés. Old Havana is being turned into a tropical Montmartre, bustling with crowds drawn by its atmosphere and fine architecture, where buildings restored to their colonial splendor are now sought-after locations for new tourist facilities and stores.

At the heart of the town is the imposing 18th-century cathedral, recently restored, and its fine square. Once deserted, it is now crowded with stalls selling craft products and souvenirs: since the liberalization of private enterprise, swarms of street vendors have started to do business, especially in this part of the city. And the renovation work continues. The most recent building restructured is an old hotel, the Ambos Mundos, where Hemingway lived during his first visit to Cuba: the terrace on its sixth floor affords a lovely view of the old town. It may be smaller and less grand than the wonderful Hotel Nacional – where the walls of the bar are literally covered in fascinating old photos – but its intimate ambience makes it an equally pleasant place to be. There are also stalls in Plaza de Armas, a large square flanked by the Museo de la Ciudad, but the merchandise on sale here is books, particularly rare editions. Also overlooking this square are the 16th-century Real Fuerza fortress, the very oldest in the Americas, and two masterpieces of Cuban baroque: the palaces of the Segundo Cabo and of the Capitanes Generales. Every street in Havana has surprises in store, for instance the elegant colonial dwelling-places that line Obispo, Mercaderes and Oficios streets. The García Lorca Theater, along the Prado, is the city's oldest and most prestigious: the ballet company directed by Alicia Alonso performs here. The Museo Nacional in the Palacio de Bellas Artes frequently mounts exhibitions of Cuban and foreign artworks; a ground-floor room is given over to naif paintings by students. Another museum, Casa de Africa, traces the history of the first Africans brought to Cuba.

Few oceanfront promenades can compare with the lovely Malecón, swept by the waves of the Caribbean. It's sad that the façades of its pastel-colored buildings in colonial Art Nouveau style are now in disrepair, crumbling beneath the gusts of wind. On the west side of the city, immediately after Puente de Hierro, is Miramar, currently the most fashionable district of Havana. Dividing it in two is Quinta Avenida: flanking one side of this road, the longest in the city, are colonial villas and embassies; on the other, hotels and discothèques. Many years ago now, Ernest Hemingway considered Cuba his home. When he wanted a drink and fancied a sweet mojito he called at La Bodeguita del Medio; for a dry daiquiri he went El Floridita instead. In spite of their popularity with tourists, Havana's two most famous bars have lost none of their character and appeal:

22 top *In Cuba every occasion can be a pretext for having fun: here* joie de vivre *is fortunately not in short supply. Even simply posing for a photo can a source of elation. These girls' amber-colored skin points to their mixed descent: Indians, Spaniards, Africans and Asians have all played a part in the island's history, creating a melting-pot of races that eventually learnt to live peacefully side by side.*

22 bottom *Cuba has about twenty million inhabitants, and a fifth of them live in Havana. As in most developing countries, the birth rate is high. In terms of racial groups, the population is comprised of 47% mulattos, 40% whites, 12% blacks and 1% Chinese. Visitors to Cuba are struck by seeing so many children and adolescents but with 50% of the population aged under 20, it's hardly surprising.*

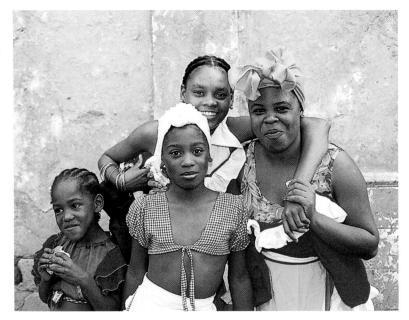

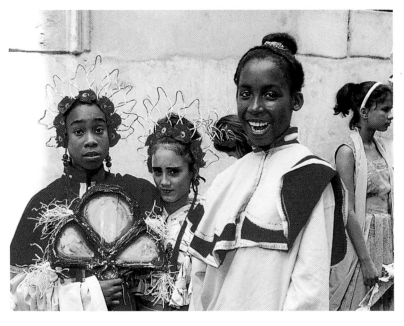

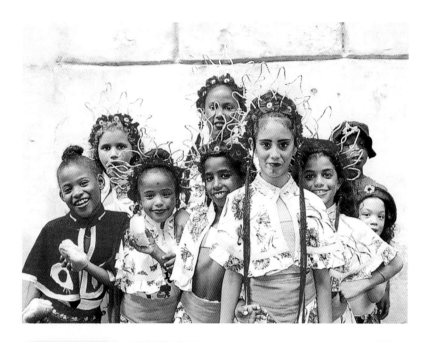

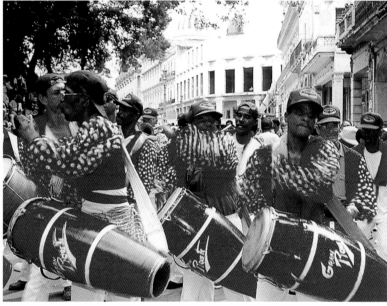

23 top *For these little girls a Chinese costume is just fancy dress but some of them may actually be of oriental descent. More than 120,000 Chinese from the Canton region emigrated to Cuba in the second half of the 19th century. Havana has its own Chinatown and only one other Latin-American country, Peru, has such a large oriental community. Cuba's Chinese immigrants fought with honor in the island's wars of independence.*

23 bottom *In Cuba people normally work five days a week. There are public holidays on January 1st (Liberation Day and Anniversary of the Revolution), May 1st (Labor Day), July 25/26/27th (Anniversary of the attack on the Moncada Garrison), October 10th (Anniversary of the start of the Wars of Independence). In July or August, carnivals are held to celebrate the end of the summer* zafra, *the sugarcane harvest.*

the first unpretentious, the second more sophisticated. Clubs and discos have instead fallen into line with international taste: in Havana there's the Tropicana, where performers and costumes change but the cabaret always seems the same, the Salòn Rojo, the Parisièn at the Hotel Nacional, the Palacio de la Salsa at the Hotel Riviera and the1830, better known as "Milocho", between Vedado and Miramar; at Varadero, the Cueva del Pirata; or, back in Havana, the Bamba and the Havana Club, where fun-seekers could be forgiven for thinking they were in Rimini or Ibiza.

West of Havana is tobacco land, a seemingly never-ending expanse of fields where tobacco for the famous Cuban cigars is grown. The plantations center on the provinces of Pinar del Río and Villa Clara, and the Viñales valley. People have always gone to Cuba to buy cigars but in recent years smoking cigars rather than cigarettes has become fashionable and demand has soared. The most popular brand is Cohibas, which, outside Cuba, can be found only in Switzerland. Other much sought-after labels of Cuba's "gold" are Monte Cristo, Romeo y Julieta, Partagas, Upmann and Diplomatic. The so-called *puros* (known abroad as Havana) are hand-rolled from Vuelta Abajo, dark tobacco considered the world's finest. Each hectare of plantation yields 40,000 plants and yet Cuba's annual production satisfies only part of world demand. The plants, which grow to the height of a man, each provide sufficient leaves for about six cigars. Making cigars is a precision operation that calls for few tools but great manual dexterity. On a bench the *torcedor* spreads the 'binder' leaves, which have been moistened in linen cloths. After trimming the edges, he rolls filler leaves inside them, then pressing the cigar in the *chaveta*, a wooden vice, to give it the correct shape. The most skilful *torcedores* produce as many as 180 cigars a day.

East of Havana, along the Via Blanca, the coastal road that links the capital with Varadero, are the golden beaches of Playas del Este, sloping gently down into the transparent waters of the ocean. These beaches – Santa Maria del Mar, Guanabo and Jibacoa, furthest from the city – are the traditional Sunday destination of the Habaneros. Just 6 miles from Havana is the fishing village of Cojímar, made famous by Ernest Hemingway in his novel "The Old Man and the Sea". The American writer paid frequent visits to this village, which was close to a house he had bought: Finca La Vigia, as the house was called, is now a museum of Hemingway memorabilia.

Varadero is situated 87 miles from Havana, on a peninsula that, although only a few hundred feet wide, stretches over 12 miles into the sea. Until the 1930s this area was practically uninhabited: there was nothing but the occasional fisherman's hut and a few isolated villas. The idea of developing a prestigious beach resort here came from the American millionaire Dupont (the villa he had built here is now the Las Americas restaurant). Before long Varadero started to grow and continued to do so until the early 1960s. In more recent years, after Soviet aid dried up and Cuba realized the tourist trade was its best bet for economic survival, Varadero has suffered the effects of over-zealous development.

Varadero is in the province of Matanzas: on the south coast the lagoon at Guamà is celebrated for the crocodiles bred there and for a reconstructed pre-Columbian village. To the east are the sugar flats, verdant plains where sugar plantations stretch as far as the eye can see, punctuated here and there by towns: Santa Clara, Cienfuegos, Sancti Spiritus, Ciego de Avila, Camaguey. This is the rural heart of Cuba, with orchards, rice fields, vegetable fields and huge livestock farms producing meat for the home market. Santa Clara is the main town of the province of Villa Clara, a major sugar-producing center. Here you can see the Tren Blindado monument, commemorating a decisive battle of Castro's Revolution. Some 31 miles away is the town of Remedios, where there are significant testimonies to the colonial period. Nearby is the fishing village of Caibarièn: the warehouses and docks where fishermen now moor their vessels are a reminder of the days when the town was an important trading port. The local beaches fringe a promontory and there is an important sailing center here where young Cubans are trained for national and international sailing, windsurfing and canoeing events.

In the Sierra del Escambray, still in the province of Villa Clara, a tourist resort has been created on the shores of the Hanabanilla reservoir, part of a hydroelectric facility that provides Santa Clara and surrounding area with power and water. The city of Cienfuegos was founded by French settlers, a fact still evident in the urban layout with its wide streets and in the handsome neoclassical buildings – the cathedral, governor's residence and Terry Theater – that overlook Parque José Martí, the central square. Growing in the Jardìn Botànico de la Soledad, outside the city, are splendid examples of the local flora: many thousands of different plants and every species of palm tree to be found on the island.

Sancti Spiritus, capital of the province of the same name, was founded in 1550. With its narrow streets and squat buildings, their windows protected by wrought-iron gratings, the city's appearance has changed little through the centuries.

Close to the island's southern shores is Trinidad, a beautiful little town founded by Diego Velázquez in 1514 (making it the third oldest settlement on Cuba, after Baracoa and Bayamo). Although the town prospered between 1600s and 1700s, it was later forgotten, far from the island's main lines of communication. It was from the town's port, Castilda, that the Spanish fleet set sail to conquer Mexico in 1518. In the 17th and 18th centuries Trinidad was plundered on numerous occasions by corsairs and English soldiers. In the 19th century it was made the capital of Cuba's central region. At that time sugarcane production resulted in a thriving economy but after the abolition of slavery, owners sold off their plantations to the peasants and emigrated. Decline set in and was not halted until after the Revolution. Today Trinidad is a gem set on the slopes of the Sierra de Escambray, a splendid heirloom of the colonial era, with baroque palaces, gardens and pastel-colored houses. Thanks to a meticulous and still ongoing restoration operation, many of its buildings are once more clad in the warm pastel shades of yellow, pink, blue and green that typically graced their façades in the 18th century.

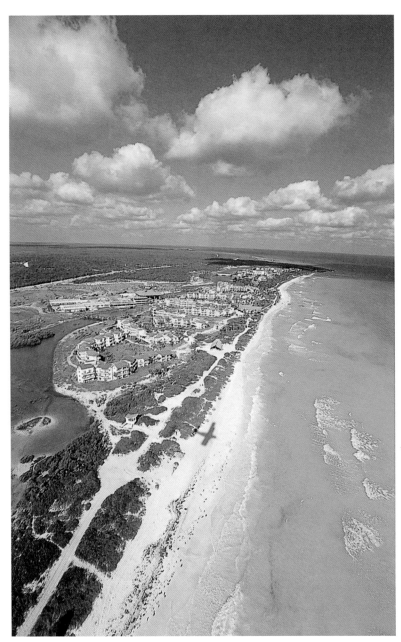

24   *An aerial view of the island of Cayo Coco. Close to the beach, the water is turquoise blue but has a sparkling, milky hue. A short way further out its color suddenly changes – seemingly along a clear-cut line – to a much deeper blue. The beach is made of fine white sand. In the illustrious club of heavenly tropical resorts dotted about the globe, Cayo Coco deserves a special place of its very own.*

25 top *Beyond all doubt Cayo Coco is the loveliest place in Ciego de Avila province. This little island with its dazzlingly white beaches is linked to the mainland by a 14-mile causeway that fringes the ocean. It is part of the archipelago of Camaguey, formed of over 800 cays and coral reefs that stretch for 248 miles, making this barrier one of the world's most important.*

25 bottom *A tourist village now welcomes vacationers to Cayo Coco. This and Cayo Giullermo are the only islands of the archipelago of Camaguey on which developers have been allowed to build hotels, in keeping with restrictions imposed to protect the environment. Tourism has nonetheless expanded rapidly on these cays and, in terms of number of visitors catered for, their structures are among the largest in Cuba.*

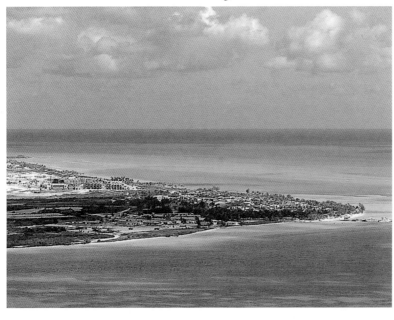

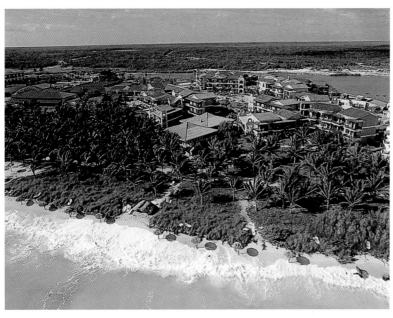

Through low windows protected by wrought-iron, it is possible to catch a glimpse of panelled ceilings, walls finished with azulejos from Seville, the ubiquitous rocking chair and shady patios embellished with lush tropical vegetation. The sloping streets are cobbled, cars are few and far between, the light is magical and the atmosphere created by a past whose architectural language centered on harmony of form and color. As in Plaza Mayor, for example: in its midst is a garden with palm trees, elaborately worked iron benches and colored terracotta vases; overlooking the square are the Museo Romantico, the church of the Santissima Trinità, the Museo de Architectura Colonial and the convent of San Ferdinando. The Museo Romantico is housed in the former home of the Brunet family, wealthy sugar plantation owners; the museum is presented as a colonial residence, containing period furniture and collections. The building now occupied by the Museo de Architectura also belonged to a rich family, the Sanchez Iznaga: its exhibits include documents on the urban planning of Trinidad and on the restoration works started in 1959. Other interesting buildings now house the Casa de la Trova, in Calle Lumumba, and the Canchànchara (named after a drink made with rum): Cuban and Afro-Cuban bands perform in its courtyard.

About 9 miles from Trinidad, emerging from the midst of fields of sugarcane, is the tall Torre de Iznaga, a watchtower built to oversee slaves at work in the fields. On the coast, not far from the old port of Casilda, is Playa Ancòn: over 6 miles of fine sands, popular with divers who go searching the coral sea bed for turtles and crustaceans.

Ciego de Avila is another important city: capital of the province of the same name, it is surrounded by fairly monotonous countryside, where agricultural production centers on sugarcane. Off the coast, in the south of the province, is the splendid archipelago of the Jardines de la Reina, also known as Laguna de la Leche on account of the milky color of the sea water, caused by its high calcium content.

One of Cuba's most densely populated cities is Camaguey, at the center of a cattle farming region considered the island's wild "far west". In the old part of the town there are some interesting baroque monuments: the cathedral, the church of Nuestra Senora de la Soledad and the building now used as the city's law courts. The strange, enormous goatskin bags seen along the streets are known as *tinajones*: they were once used to collect rainwater. In Camaguey as in Trinidad there is an old Casa de la Trova, where these special traditional Cuban ballads can be heard sung. Extending north of the city is the Sierra de Cubitas, where caves with rock drawings done by pre-Columbian Indians have been discovered. Skirting the northern coastline is the Archipelago de Camaguey; the largest of its countless islets are Cayo Romano and Cayo Sabinal. From Victoria de las Tunas there are two roads that both lead to Santiago de Cuba: the main one is the continuation of the Carretera Central, the other route takes travelers through Bayamo and across Granma province. Further along the central highway is Holguìn, traditionally believed to be the site of Cubanacàn (meaning "center of Cuba"), the village visited by Christopher Columbus on his first journey to the New World. The slopes of Loma de la Cruz offer a fine vantage point for panoramic views of the city and surrounding area. The second route heads towards Bayamo, the capital of Granma province, named after the yacht with which, in 1956, Fidel Castro and his supporters landed at Playa Las Coloradas. This was the start of the revolutionary exploits that took them first into the maze of rainforests and rugged mountains of the Sierra Maestra, whose foothills stretch as far as the eastern tip of the island. The only way to get around in this part of the island is often on narrow roads that wind through thick forests, interrupted by occasional clearings and villages. Nestling at the foot of the Sierra is Santiago, permanently swathed in clouds of tropical moisture. The city is famous for its carnival, dating from the colonial era when it was held in January on the feast-day *de los reyes,* and black slaves were allowed to dance in the streets. The carnival now takes place in mid-July, at the end of the *zafra,* the sugarcane harvest. Santiago was founded by the Spanish in 1514 and was Cuba's capital until 1549. Thanks to its sheltered natural harbor on the shores of the Caribbean, it became the main center of the island's thriving slave trade. After the Spanish surrendered to the Americans in 1898 and the new government was established in Havana, the city's importance gradually declined. It is nonetheless still considered a heroic city, cradle of the Revolution and stronghold of Cuban socialism. It was in fact in Santiago that the Revolution started, on July 26th 1953, with the unsuccessful attack on the Moncada garrison by Castro and his fellow rebels. And it was also here that Castro accepted the surrender of Batista's army in 1959. Santiago is populated by people of varied ethnic origin, more Caribbean than Cuban. Many Haitians who fled here in the late 18th century brought elements of a cultural heritage much influenced by the French. Although it is the island's second-largest city, Santiago has never seen the widespread urban blight suffered by Havana. With its sensual atmosphere and colonial architecture – its buildings finished with intricately worked wrought-iron balconies, gratings and gates – it is the acknowledged home of Cuba's great musical tradition.

Further east is Guantanamo, site of an American naval base: even after the Revolution, the U.S. has continued to maintain a garrison here, as a consequence of earlier treaties and, in particular, the Platt Amendment that, at the end of the war of independence, gave the United States the right to intervene in Cuba's defence.

Practically at the easternmost tip of the island is Baracoa, yet another rich testimony to the colonial era. Beyond the town, against the imposing backdrop offered by Yunque, the sacred mountain whose peak rarely emerges from the clouds, there are rainforests that resemble the tropical forests of the Amazon and wooden houses practically enveloped in vegetation. Founded in 1512, Baracoa was the first Spanish settlement in Cuba; like Trinidad, the 20th century it has experienced decades of isolation and is now seemingly frozen in the past.

Today Cuba has a population of over twenty million people, sprung from a variegated – but mainly African and Spanish – amalgam of cultures. Descendants of Europeans, Africans and Asians too embody the spirit of this warm, inviting land. Much of their reverie originates far far away, sometimes nurtured by ingenuity and

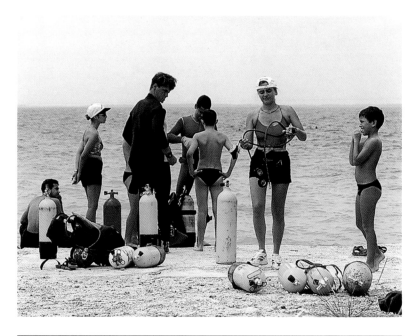

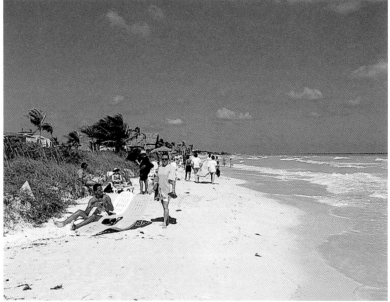

26 top *Fine white sand, crystal-clear water, miles of coral reefs populated by fish of every color imaginable: the earthly paradise offered by the Caribbean is only a few steps away from the holiday village. The days are filled mainly with* tomar el sol y bucear, *sunbathing and diving. Divers are often earlier risers, irresistibly attracted by the exploration of underwater caves surrounded by huge sponges and reef walls covered with coral fans.*

26 bottom *The other traditional pastime in tourist villages – considered* de rigueur *for holidaymakers – is* tomar el sol, *and indeed, nothing could be more pleasurable than alternating the warm caresses of the sun with refreshing*

dips in translucent sea water. The beaches of Cayo Coco are unpretentious strips of powder-like sand, lapped by gentle waves and fringed by low vegetation. The heat of the tropics is often attenuated by the softly blowing Trade Winds.

27 *For anyone who loves the sea, Cuba offers countless opportunities for such sports as swimming, diving and windsurfing. There's always a breeze and the sea has just the right amount of swell to make for thrilling "roller rides", either in the more subdued light of morning or in the brilliant afternoon sunshine, when the enveloping silence is broken only by waves breaking on the shore.*

28-29 A small tourist plane projects its shadow on the lush green vegetation covering one of the cays.
Along the submerged continental platform opposite the shores of Ciego de Avila and Camaguey are hundreds of these tiny, uninhabited islands, clearly visible amid clear, shallow waters. Some are home to iguanas that roam freely in the ground-hugging vegetation, others to crocodiles.

30-31 Few cities in Latin America have greater charm than Trinidad, with its many testimonies to the Spanish colonial era. Handsome buildings, narrow cobbled streets, patios adorned with tropical plants, wrought-iron grills on tall windows, fragrant flowers and a pervading atmosphere of the past; so much to delight visitors and tempt them to prolong their stay in a town where sounds, light and color add to the picturesque urban scene.

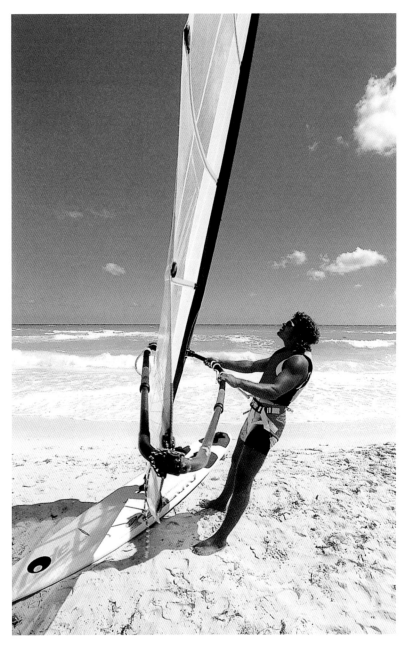

illusions, sometimes by a pragmatic view of utopia. Their dreams mix and merge on the white beaches of the Tropics, in the languid charm of Havana, in the swaying hips and African rhythms of Santiago, in rum-soaked music, and in air that sticks to the skin like sugarcane molasses. Admittedly the wind of change is blowing across Cuba. But the island still has its same irresistible charm, its intoxicating cocktail of colonial atmosphere and tropical setting, romantic beaches and sensual pleasures, music (from salsa to the latest rock), new wave films and young writers, exotic cruises and villages beyond the reach of civilization. In the last few years, almost in step with its increasing economic difficulties, Cuba's spiritual awareness has mushroomed, further accentuated by the long awaited and eventually granted visit from Pope John Paul II.

Predominating among the various faiths and rites professed and practised in Cuba is Santería, combining Roman Catholicism with African beliefs. Ceremonies take place in the presence of a Bambalau, a kind of priest who officiates in private homes. Some 70% of the island's population are believed to follow this Afro-Cuban religion. Medicinal herbs, amulets, lucky charms and palos to ward off the evil eye are in plentiful supply in the shops of the *yerberos*, found mainly around the market of Cuatro Caminos, between Matadero and Monte, in Old Havana. And their buyers are solely Cubans, of every age and social class.

Possibly now most prominent among the many aspects of the island is its new importance as a tourist destination. Its beautiful sea, clean beaches and affordable exotic appeal have attracted millions of visitors, especially to the numerous villages where the price paid for a package holiday really is all-inclusive. The villages are built in stunning positions, with due respect for the natural environment; they are often completely isolated but totally self-sufficient, served by roads and tiny airports with air strips long enough for the small planes used for excursion flights to the loveliest tourist areas. They are often situated in the midst of nature reserves (but a constant watch is kept on the delicate equilibrium of the surrounding environment). The village formula is an undeniable success: not only are the facilities offered excellent, the staff speak foreign languages and, especially, the "national" language of the village. People who choose this kind of holiday see it as the hassle-free option, with assistance on hand from the moment of departure to arrival back home. This is one of the ways, and perhaps the easiest, to enjoy Cuba as "paradise on earth": for these tourists, Isla Grande is an island like many others, an idyllic Caribbean spot that is only sea, beaches, and palm trees. However, Cuba is actually much more than a simple vacation destination. Its history, diverse plant and wildlife, and the ethnic mix that characterizes its population gives the country the charm of a place out of the ordinary. Visiting it, getting to know its people, and speaking with the many Cubans willing to share confessions and personal stories, the sweetness, optimism, and sense of solidarity of a people that have never lost sight of the difference between being and having can be discovered. This is the important lesson for life to be learned from exploring Cuba and becoming acquainted – albeit superficially – with its people.

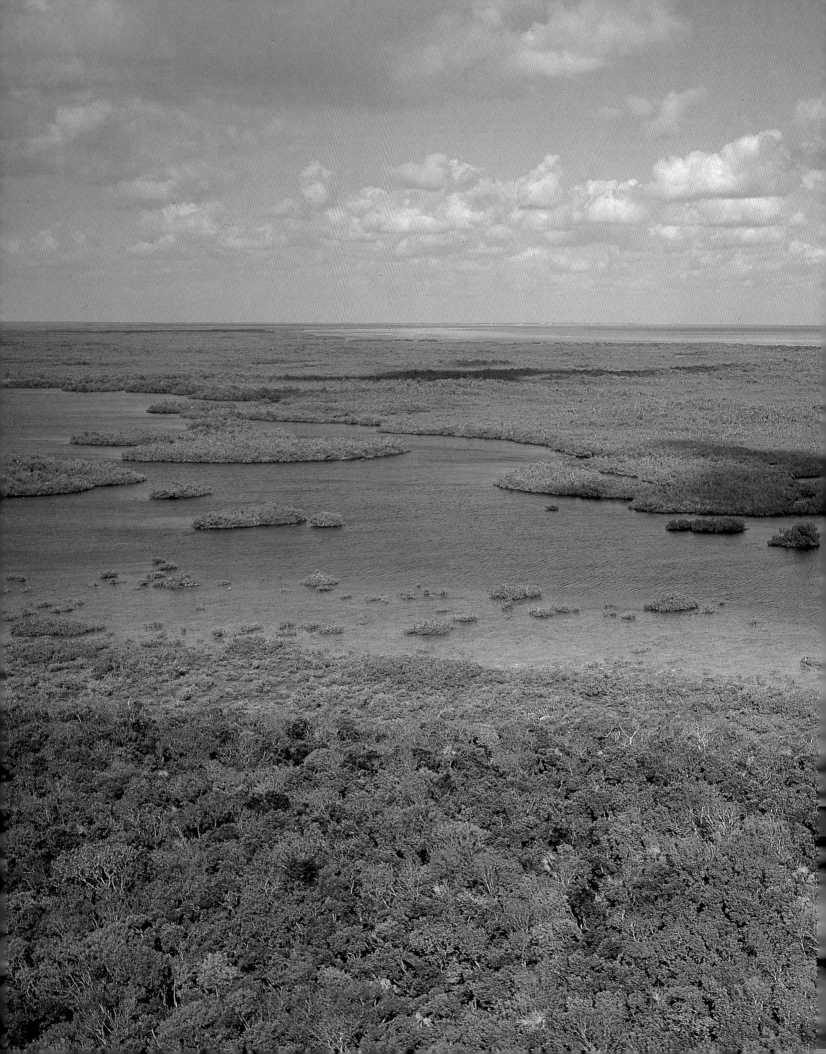

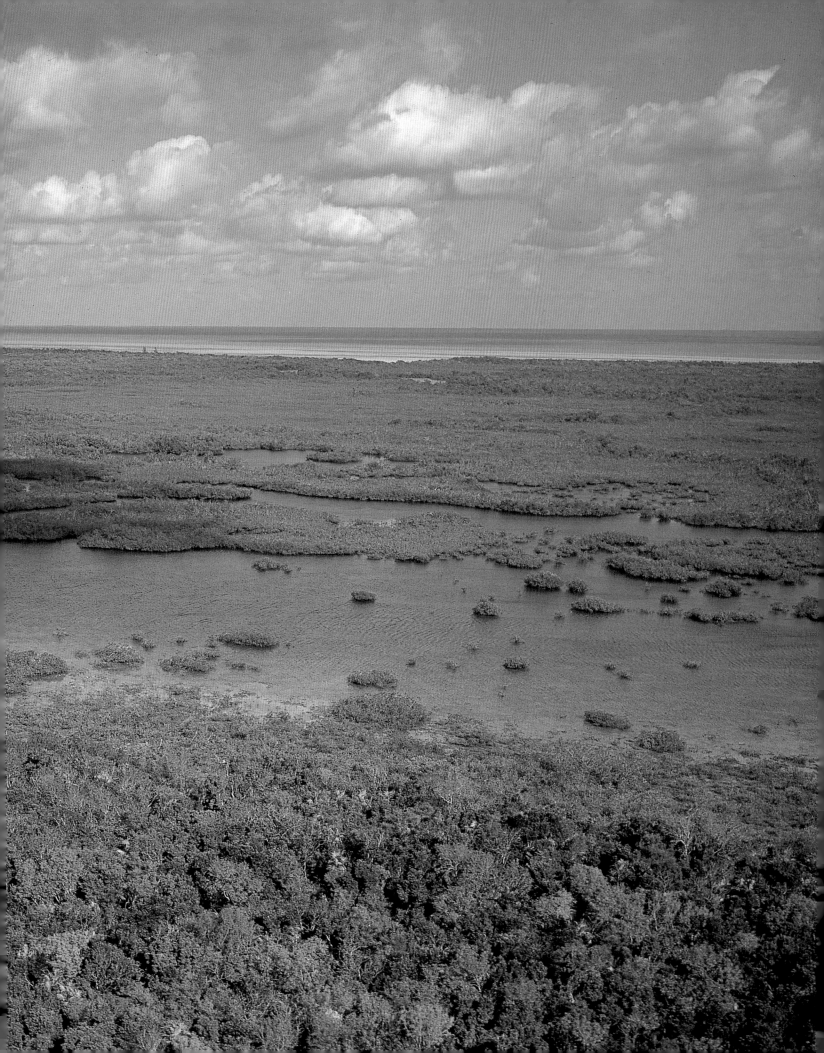

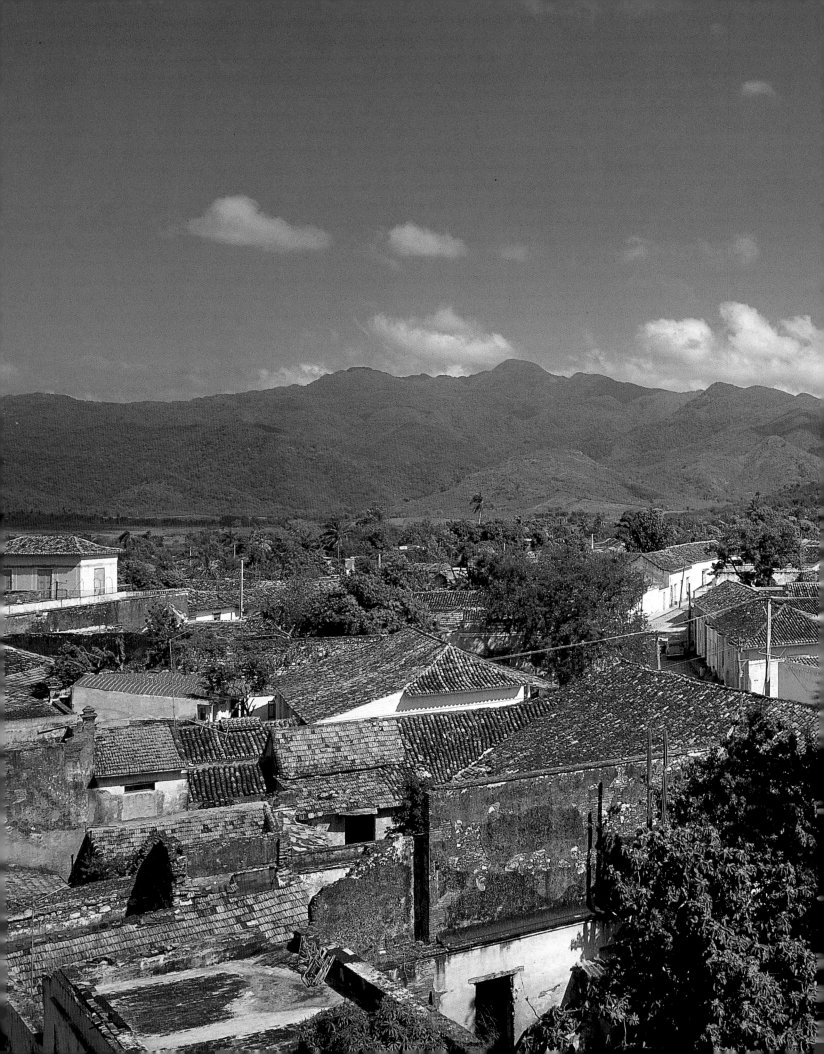

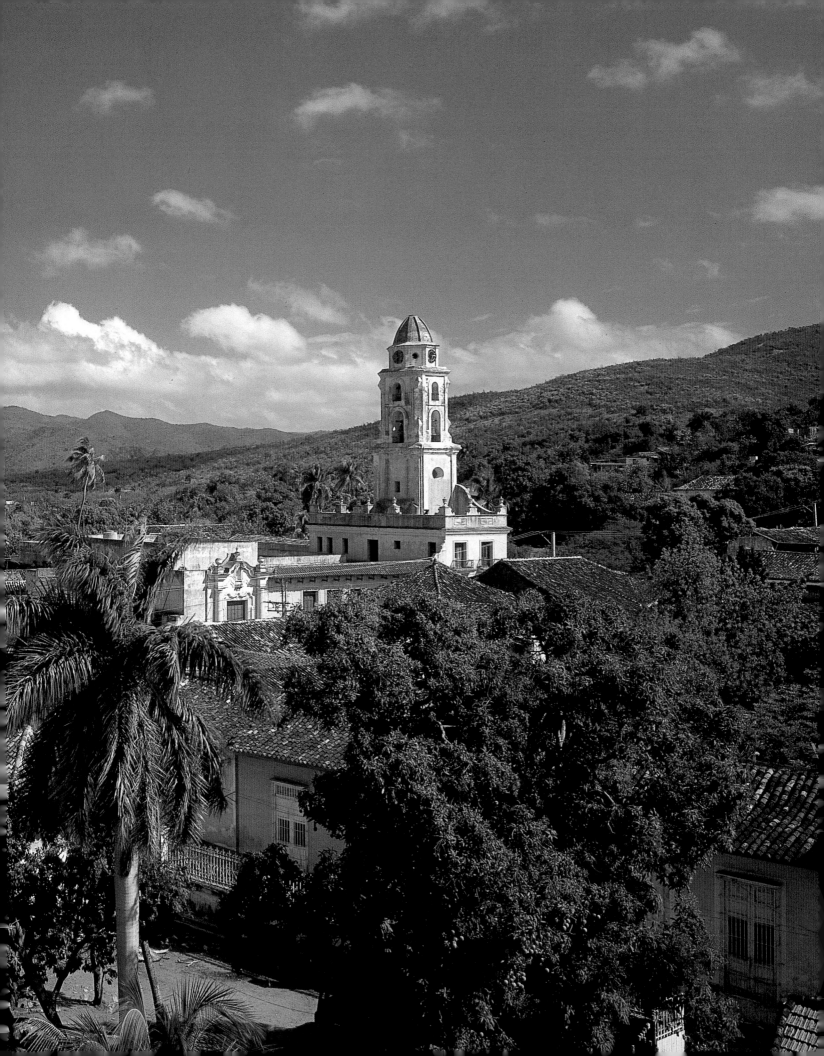

Treasures of the Antilles

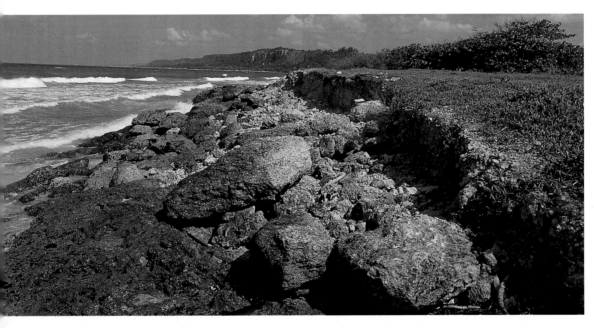

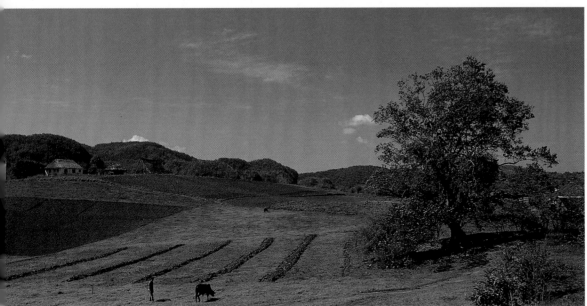

32 top *Extending for tens of miles along the coast, east of Havana, are the capital's beaches. Known as Playas del Este, the area comprises a succession of resorts including El Mégano, Santa Maria del Mar, Boca Cioga, Guanabo and Jibacoa. Behind sandy beaches interspersed with rocky bays are hotels, bungalows, restaurants, bathing establishments, discothèques, shops and water sports centers, all characterized by the same friendly and unpretentious atmosphere.*

32 bottom *A rural landscape shaped by cultivated fields and gently rolling hills greets visitors to the valley of Viñales, in Pinar del Río province. Tobacco and several varieties of fruit are grown here; vegetation is prolific, with immense orchids and amazingly tall royal palms. Punctuating the scenery are strange "haystack" hills and caverns crossed by underground streams, stunning waterfalls and rocky cliff faces where echoing voices can be heard.*

33 *Admittedly the tourist boom has brought dozens of new hotels to Varadero but its fine sandy beaches, fringed by rows of coconut palms, are still among the most beautiful on the island of Cuba. In the early years of the 20th century Varadero was an elite haven for well-heeled visitors. Development started in earnest in the '50s and is currently progressing at an unprecedented pace that has doubled or even tripled the resort's tourist structures.*

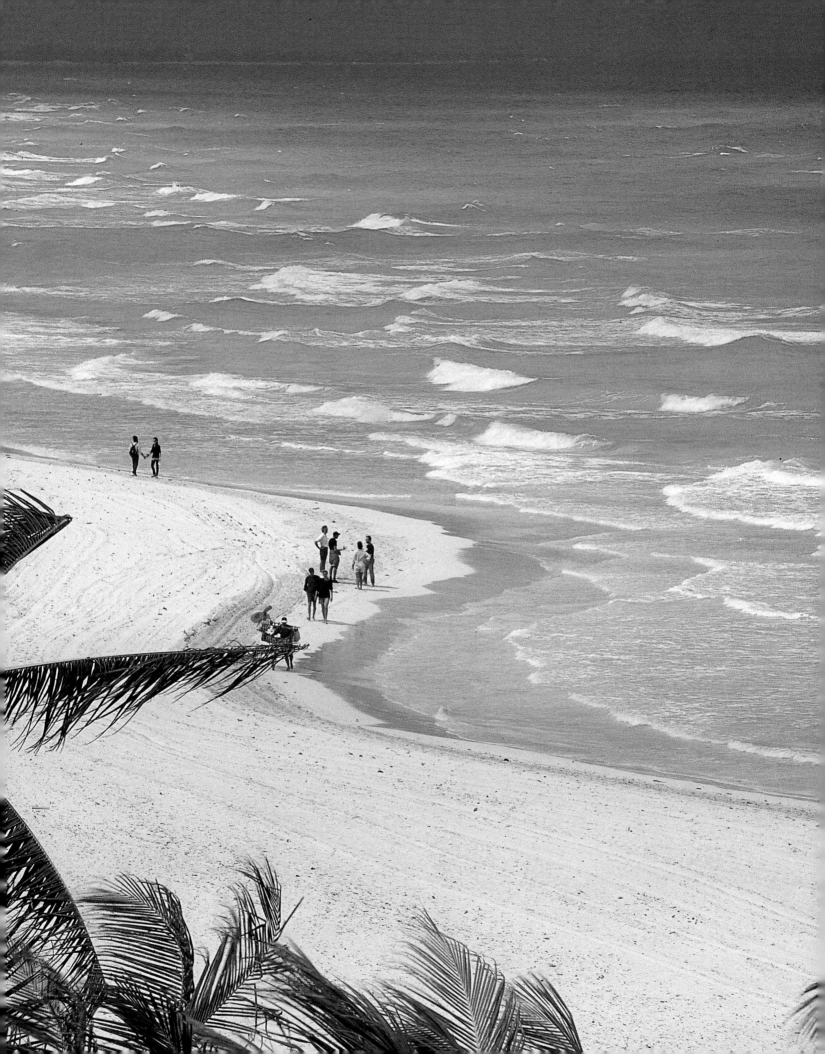

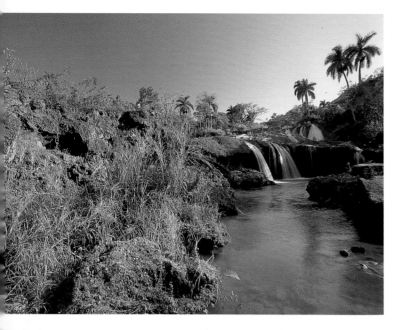

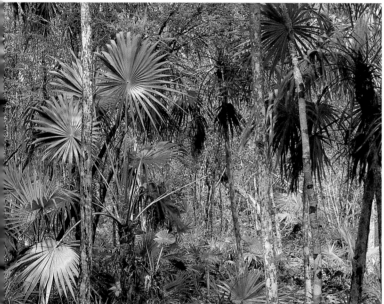

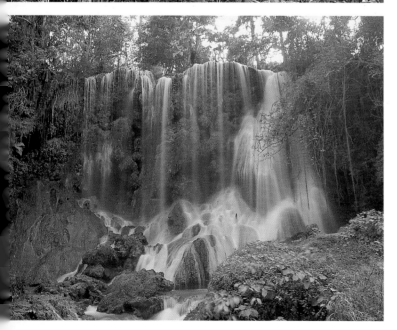

34 top *The Sierra del Escambray is generously endowed with beautiful scenery, rivers and small lakes where the water is cool and pure. Even high in these mountains vegetation is abundant thanks to the tropical climate. The road from Cienfuegos to Trinidad crosses the Sierra del Escambray (also known as Guamuhaya); it is a scenic drive, the glorious views culminating when the road emerges from the mountains and Trinidad is visible below, resplendent against the waters of the Caribbean.*

34 center *Practically hidden in dense tropical vegetation that fringes the shores of the Matanzas region are several intriguing caverns where vast quantities of fish swim in waters that spring from beneath the cave floor. The most famous and fascinating of all is the Cueva de Bellamar, just over 3 miles from the town of Matanzas: discovered in 1861, it is formed by numerous caves with stalactites, stalagmites and calcite crystals that cover the floor, walls and roof.*

34 bottom *The Cubans may refer to them with the diminutive* saltitos, *but the waterfalls of the Sierra del Escambray are much more than "little leaps". An obvious example are the falls on the region's main river, the Hanabanilla, which discharges its waters into the Embalse of the same name. This enormous reservoir, encompassed by mountains, is now a popular tourist attraction.*

34-35 *The Sierra del Escambray is one of Cuba's most impenetrable areas, one-time refuge of guerrilla groups. Along the course of many streams and rivers that descend from its rocky heights are spectacular waterfalls. The one shown in this photo is the waterfall on the Hanabanilla, an important river that feeds a reservoir.*

36-37 *On the slopes of the Sierra del Escambray, at 2,624 feet above sea level, there is a splendid nature reserve, a national park extending over an area of 43 square miles, covered with eucalyptus and pine woods. Growing along the banks of the Vega Grande river are more than 300 different plant species, from every single continent. Also part of the park is a botanical garden specializing in different varieties of coffee.*

38-39 *Dotted about the Valle de los Ingenios, close to Trinidad, are the ruins of numerous sugar mills (*ingenios *was the Spanish name for the structures where sugarcane was turned into sugar). According to the 1795 census, there were then 2,767 slaves living in the town of Trinidad. In that same year the area's 82 sugar mills produced 60,000 arrobas of sugar, almost 1,000 barrels of aguardiente and 700 jars of molasses.*

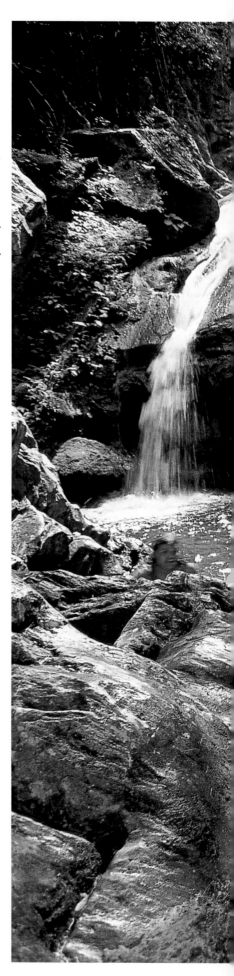

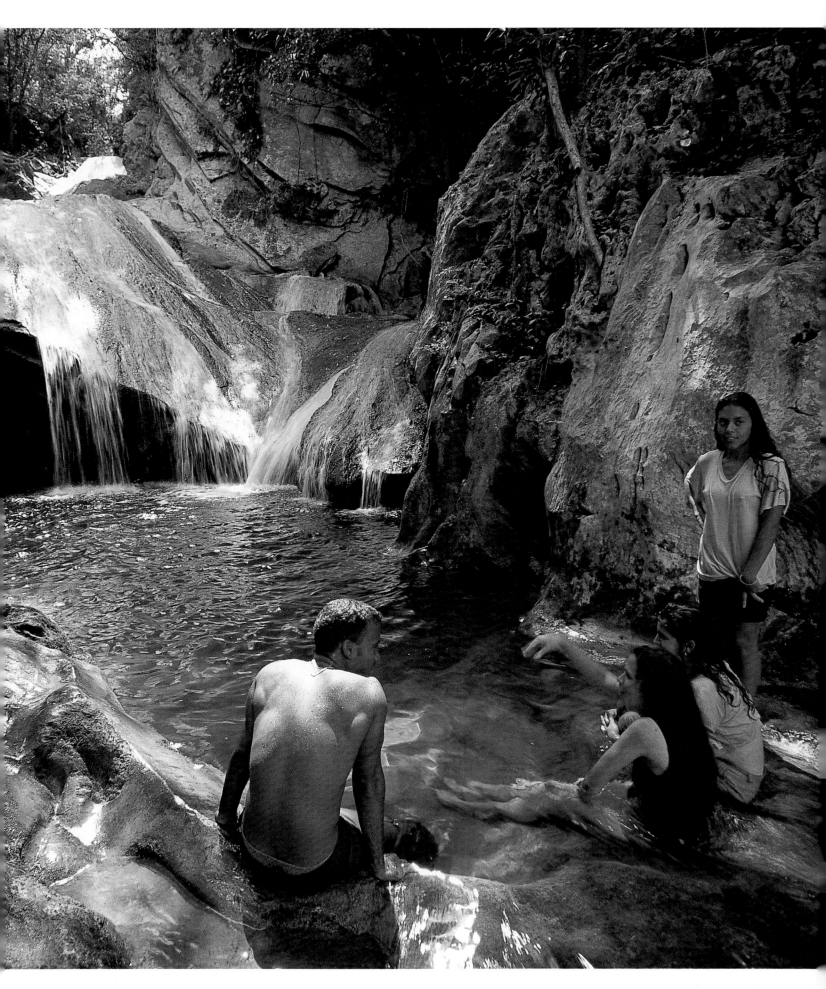

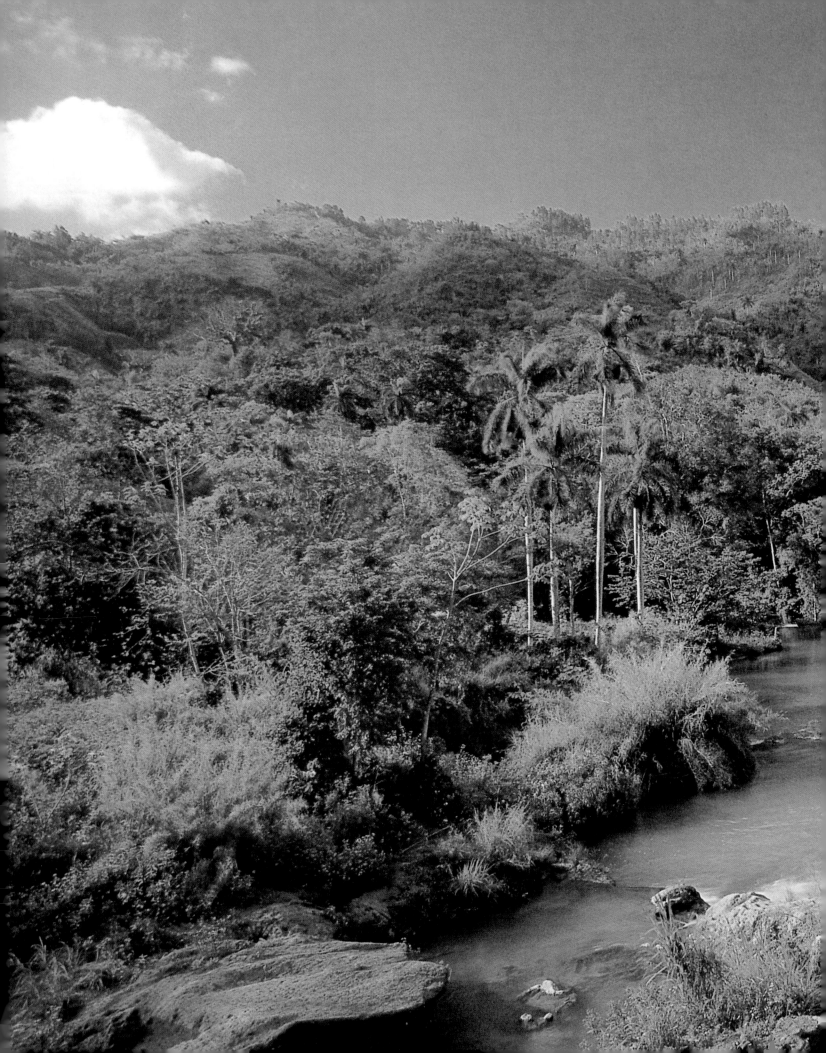

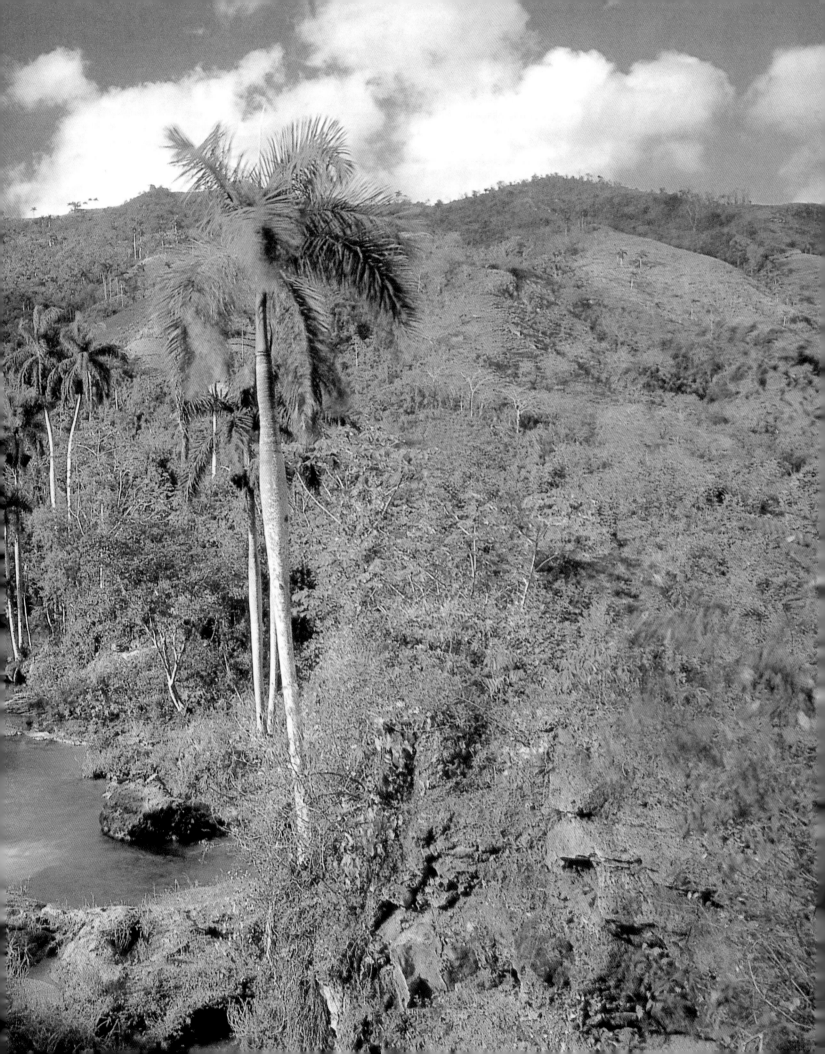

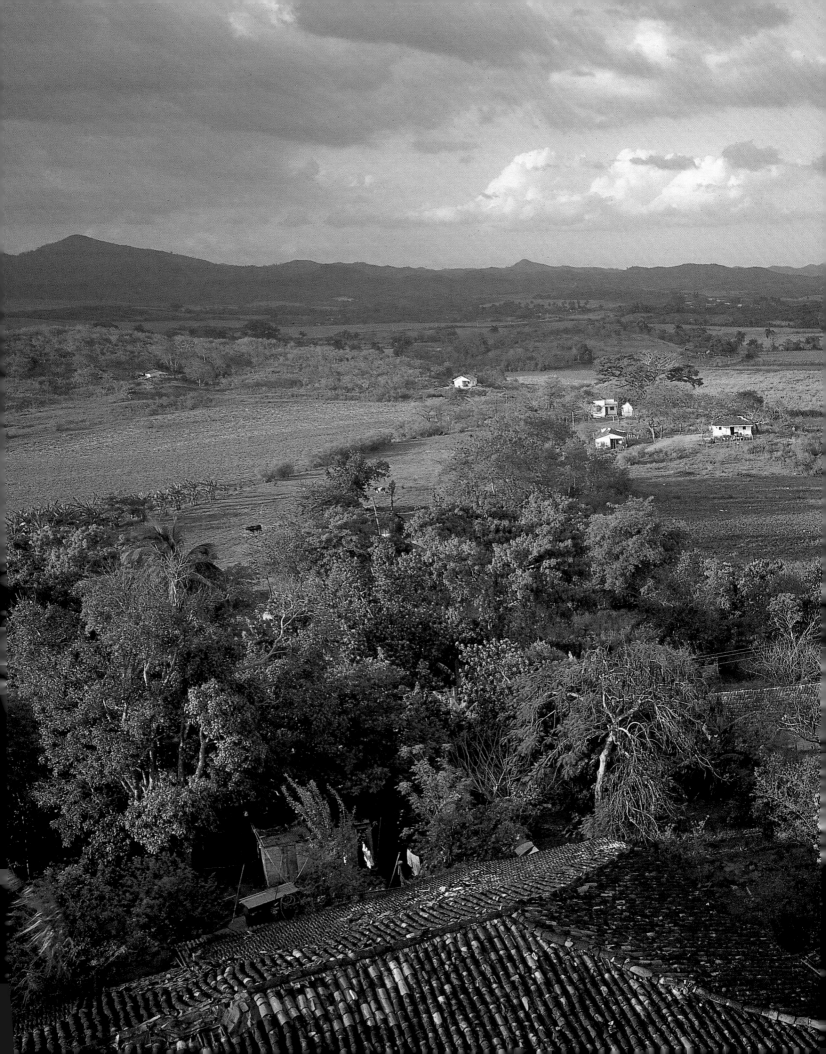

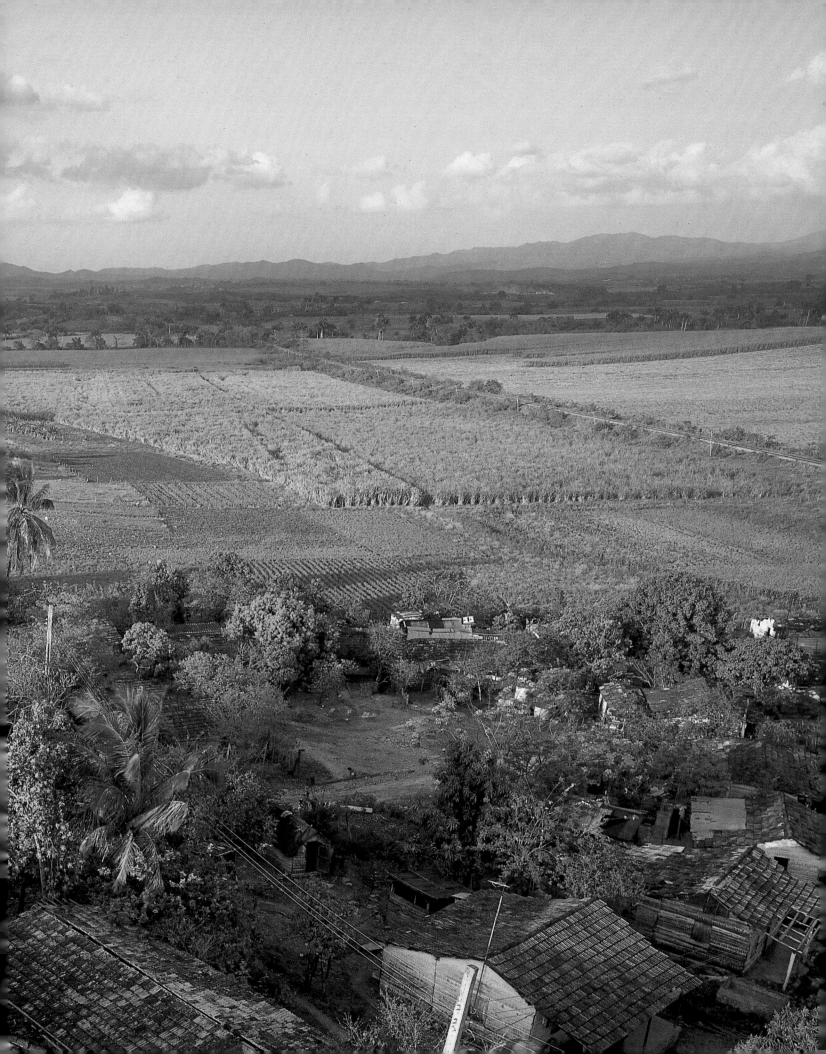

The *cuevas* of Matanzas

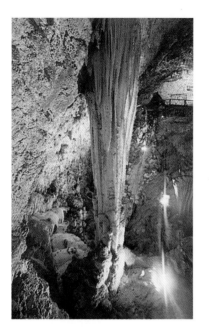

40 top *The Galleria del Confessionale is one of the most spectacular features of the Cueva de Bellamar, the most famous cavern in the Matanzas region. Reportedly found by a slave in 1861, the gallery is 577 feet long and 10 feet high and its roof is thick with stalactites. It's said that a thousand tons of rock had to be removed to unblock the entrance to the cavern. Over a mile of caves and tunnels have now been explored at this site.*

40 bottom *Perhaps the most impressive of the caves found in the Cueva de Bellar – on account of the thousands of tiny calcite crystals that cover the roof, walls and floor – is the so-called Dalie Lake.*

41 *The Cueva del Indio, in the valley of Viñales, served as both safe haven and cemetery for the Guanahatebey Indians who inhabited this area before the Conquistadores arrived on the scene. In the cavern a twisting gallery leads to an underground stream; its waters, reached down steps carved in the rock, are navigable in small boats.*

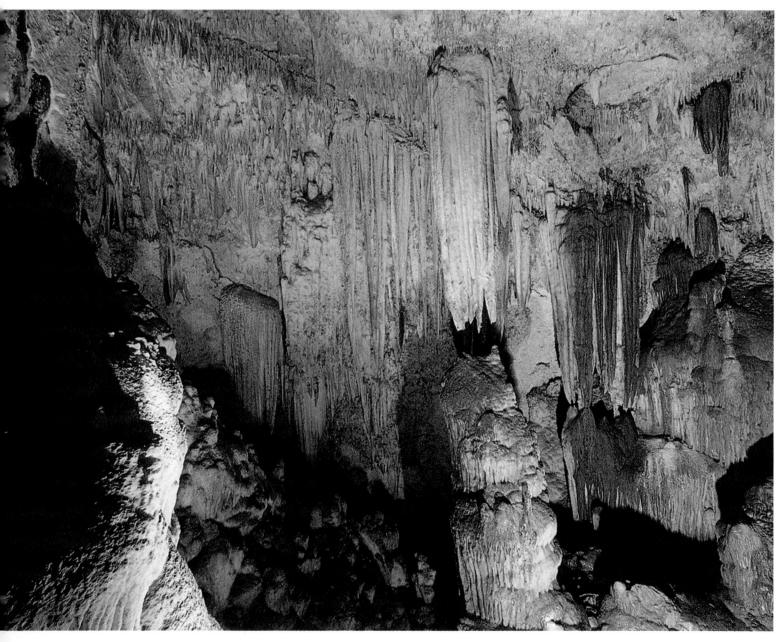

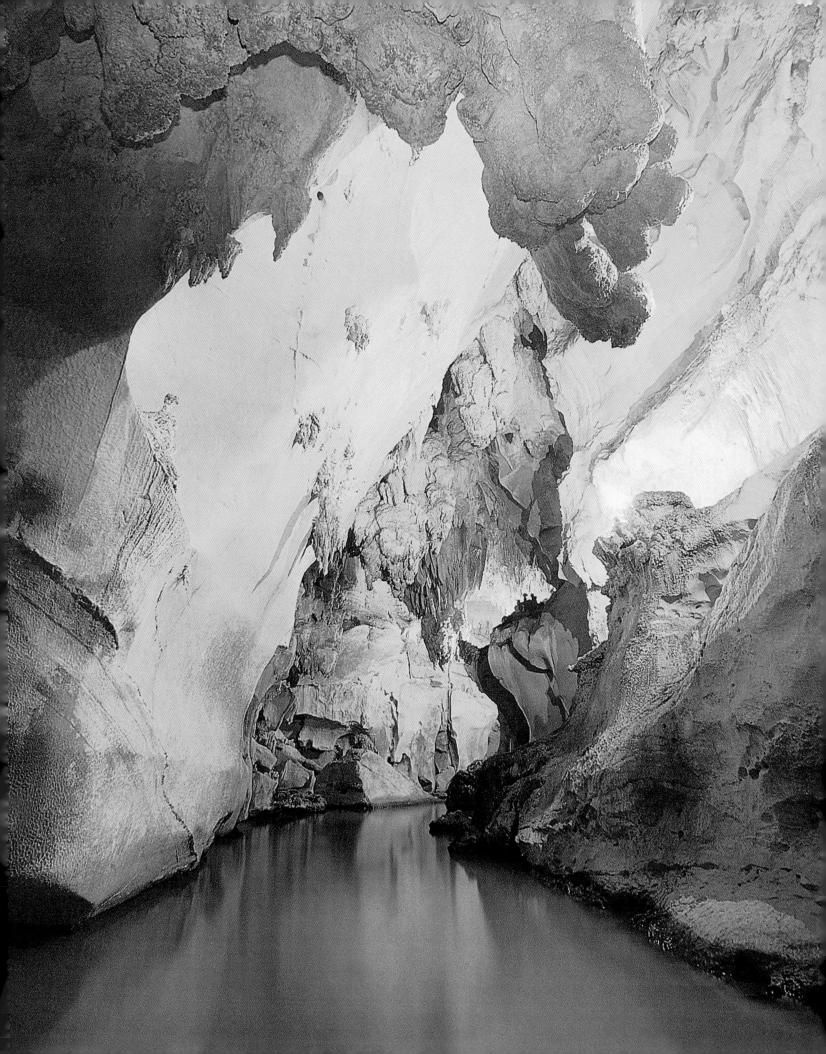

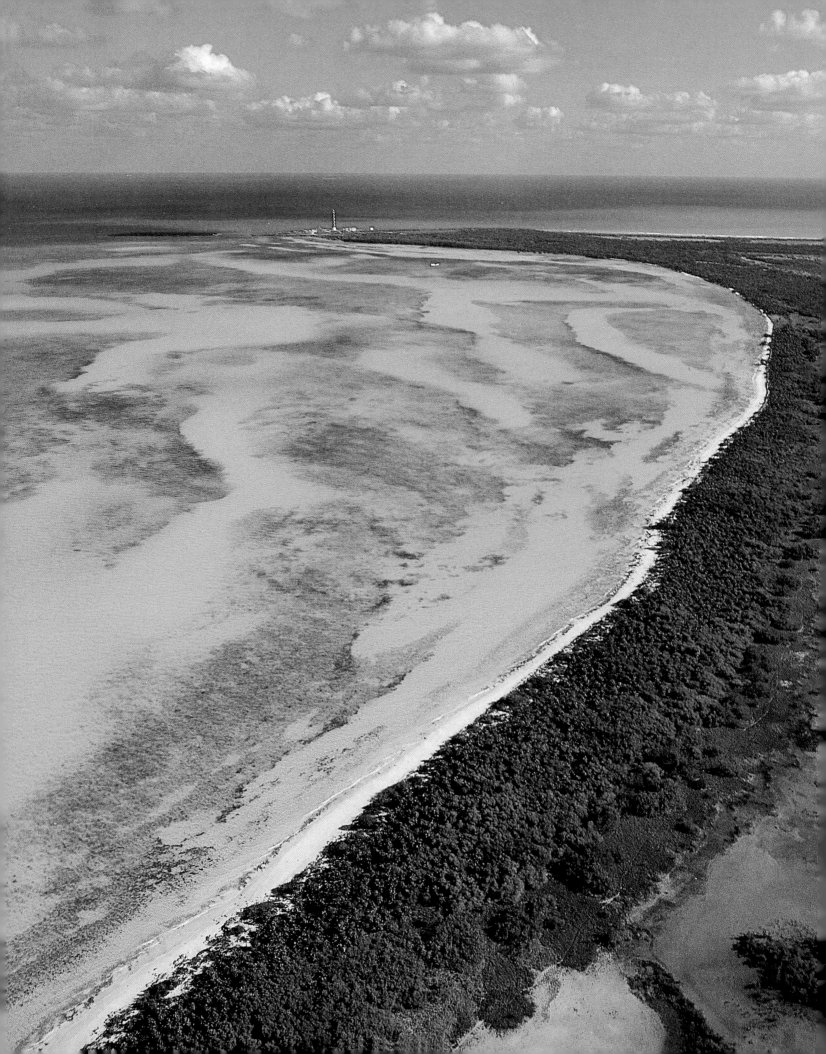

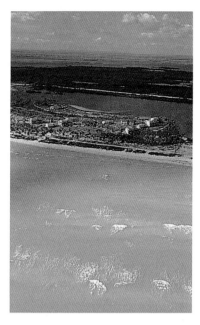

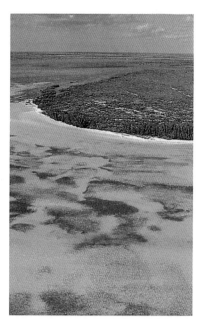

Cayo Coco, the promised land

44-45 *An aerial view of the tourist village built on the island of Cayo Coco, connected by road on the coast of Ciego de Avila, along a 14 mile long causeway, to the small town of Morón. The tourist complexes on Cayo Coco and nearby Cayo Guillermo are the only ones in existence on the vast archipelago.*

46-47 *The sun casts the clearly defined shadow of a coconut palm on the fine sand of a beach in Cayo Coco.*

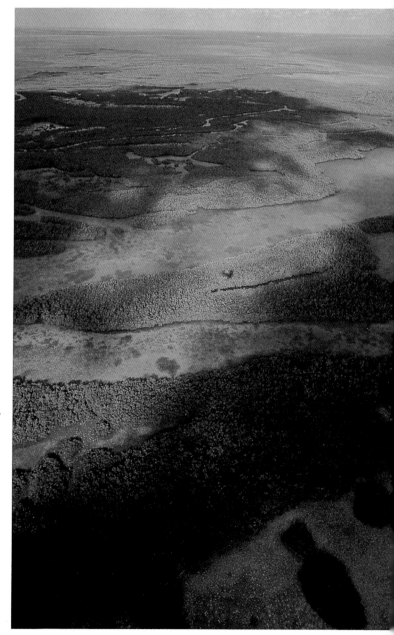

42 *Cayo Coco, off the coast of Ciego de Avila, is the largest of the area's myriad islets. In many respects its beaches are finer than those of Varadero, Cuba's foremost tourist resort. It is not named after the coconut palm, as one might have assumed, but after the local name for the white ibis, a wader of the island's most interesting birdlife species.*

43 top left *Several tourist complexes have been operating for some years on Cayo Coco and Cayo Guillermo. Since the archipelago of Camaguey has a delicate ecosystem it is vitally important that steps be taken to protect the area's natural assets.*

43 top right *This aerial photo of the island of Cayo Coco does full justice to the stunning colors of the surrounding ocean. The sand on the beaches is white and as fine as powder. A garden of Eden, so far untouched by the adverse effects of mass tourism.*

43 bottom left *Cayo Coco's heavenly white sandy beaches – there are at least nine on the island, stretching for a total of over 13 miles – make it the loveliest place in Ciego de Avila province. The archipelago of Camaguey, formed by 800 cays, is surrounded by a barrier reef extending for almost 250 miles, making it one of the most important in the world.*

43 right *The archipelago of Camaguey seen from the air. The cays are separated from one another by shallow channels of crystalline water, bright blue-green in color, through which the sea bed is clearly visible. Various wild animals inhabit these tiny islands: the wild boar, for instance, was probably introduced by pirates in recent centuries while the cays are the natural habitat of turtles, crocodiles, iguanas and waterfowl.*

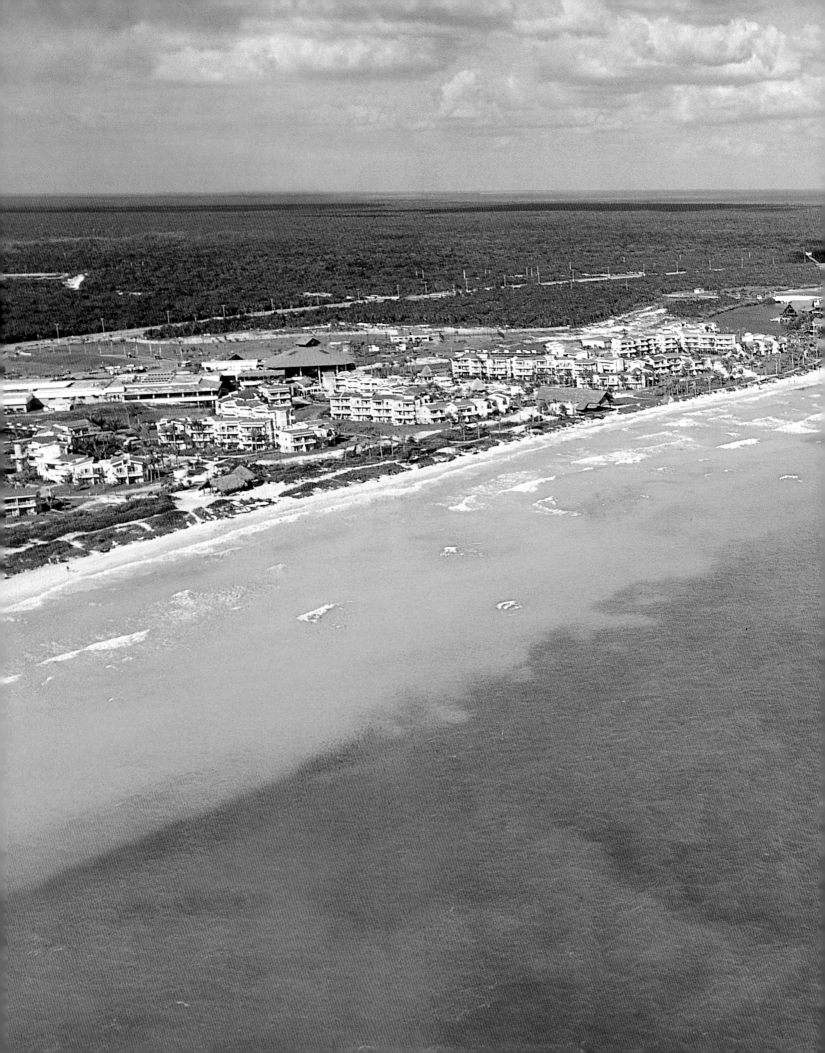

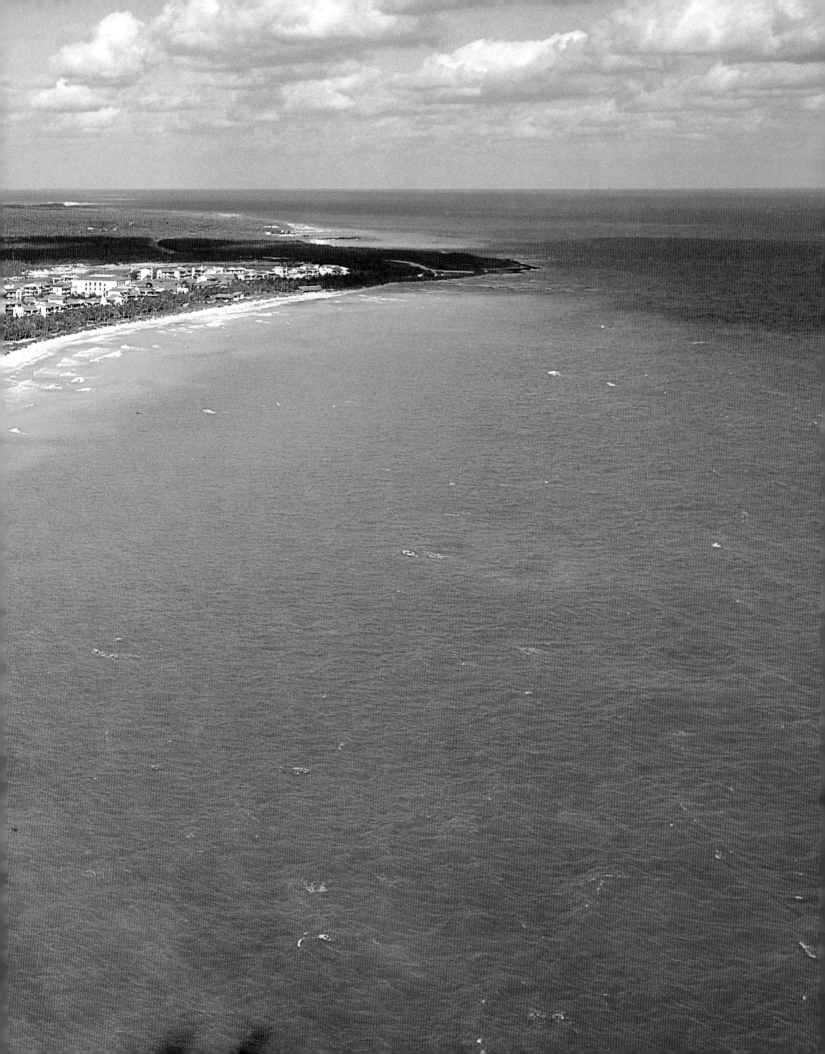

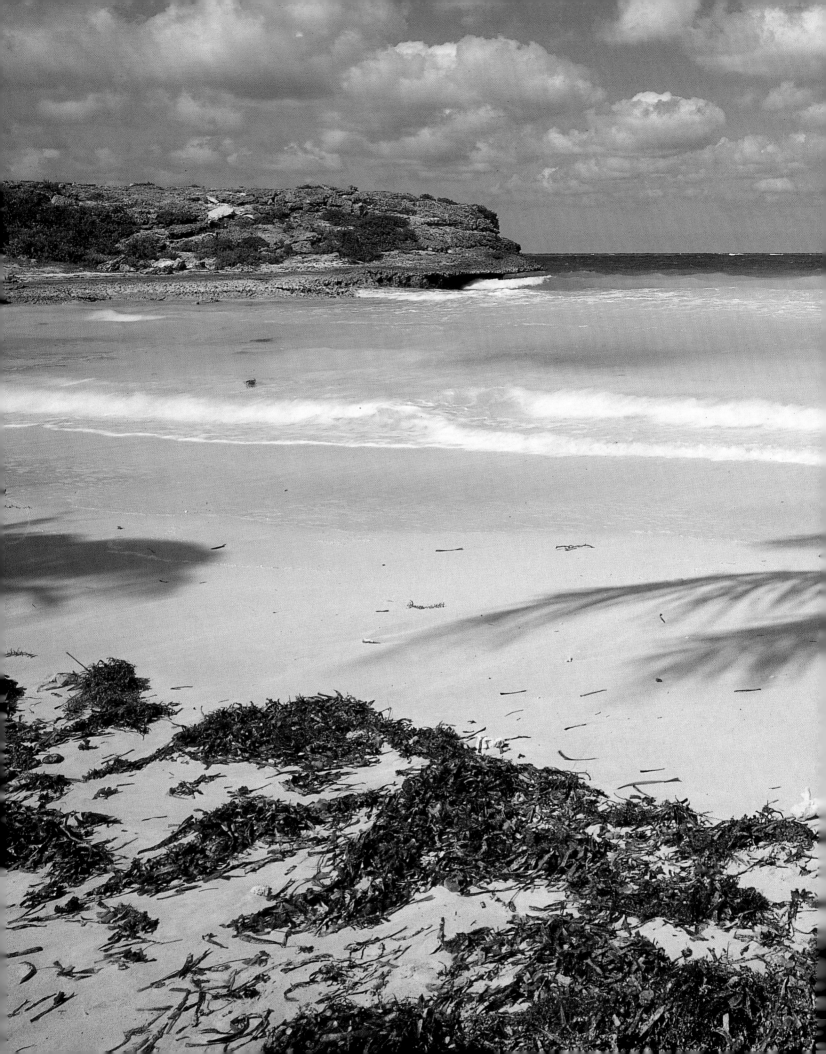

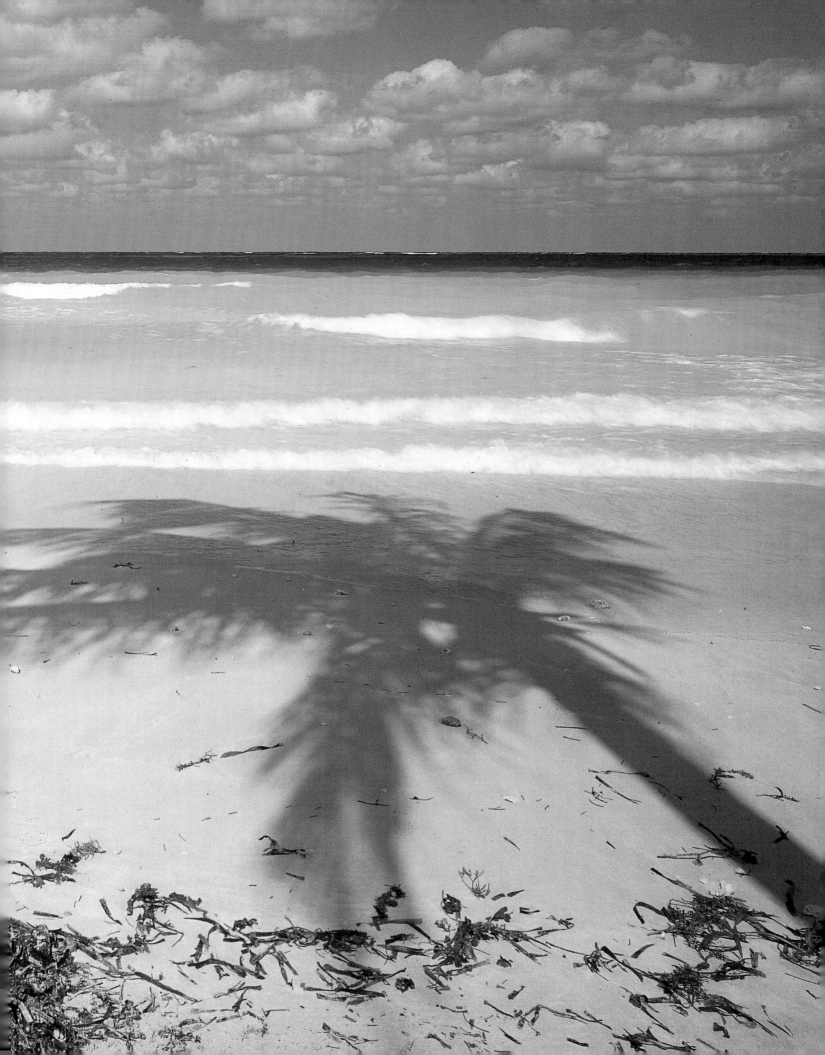

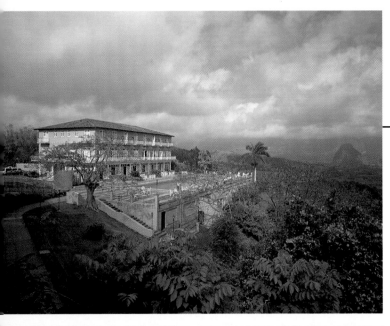

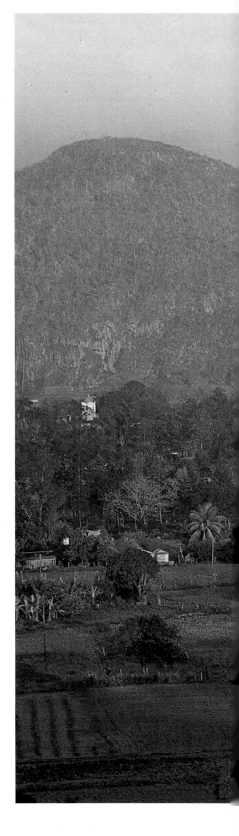

The *mogotes* of Pinar del Río

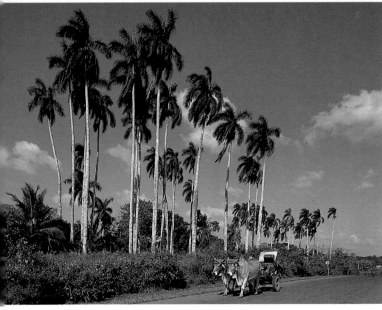

48 top *Los Jazmines is the best known hotel in the Pinar del Río region. Located on a mountain slope along the road to Pinar, about 2 miles from Viñales, it offers panoramic views of mogotes, tobacco plantations and rows of royal palms. Its salmon-pink façade and large pool are instantly visible against the lush green vegetation.*

48 center *Tall, slender royal palms are a leitmotiv of the scenery in Pinar del Río province. Their exceptional height contrasts with the flatness of the tobacco plantations but echoes the shape of the mogotes, the bizarre rock formations that emerge from cultivated fields, looking like ancient ruins hidden under dense vegetation.*

48 bottom *A tobacco farmer's hut – called a rancho – in the Pinar del Río region. In these windowless drying houses the tobacco leaves are hung on long horizontal poles, starting from the back and using every inch of available space, from wall to wall and from roof to floor. The leaves are cured for 45 days, in total darkness.*

48-49 *In prehistoric times the valley of Viñales was an enormous cavern: its roof, which subsequently collapsed, was supported by huge natural pillars, now the strange haystack-shaped hills that Cubans call mogotes. In their shade grow verdant plantations – or vegas – of the world's finest tobacco. The leaves of these plants are used to make the famous cigars referred to as tobacos by the Cubans but known to the rest of the world as Havana.*

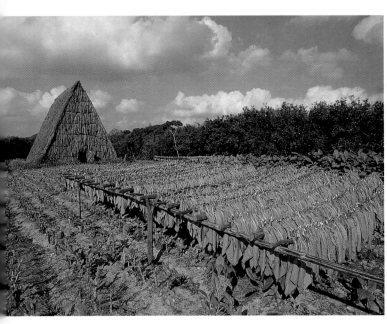

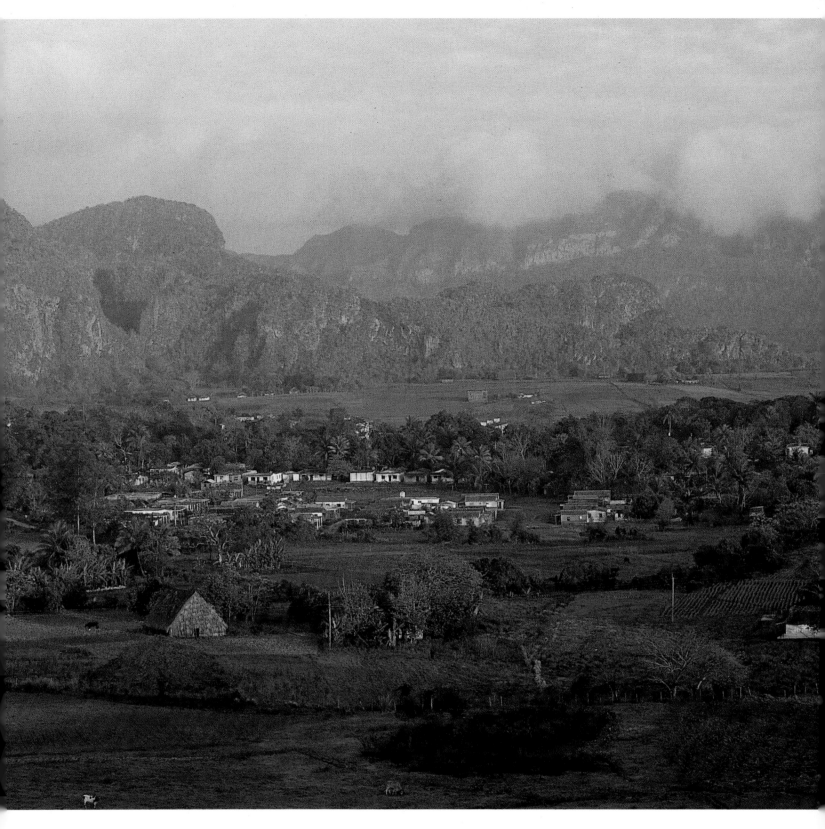

50-51 *The backdrop for the tobacco field pictured here is provided by the* mogotes, *distinctive karst "haystack" hills that are a feature of the landscape in Pinar del Río province. This whole region is ideal for growing* tobacco, *a delicate, quality crop that needs careful handling. The production process, from seed to cigar, involves over a hundred operations, almost all of them manual: rolling the cigars calls for particular dexterity and expertise.*

52-53 *Waterfalls are a major attraction in the Sierra del Escambray, the mountain range that rises up behind the city of Trinidad (and, save for a few roads winding their way across the region, is practically inaccessible). And yet peasants manage to farm patches of land here, mainly on the shores of lakes: they keep bees, raise cattle and produce most of the food they need, like fruit, vegetables and coffee.*

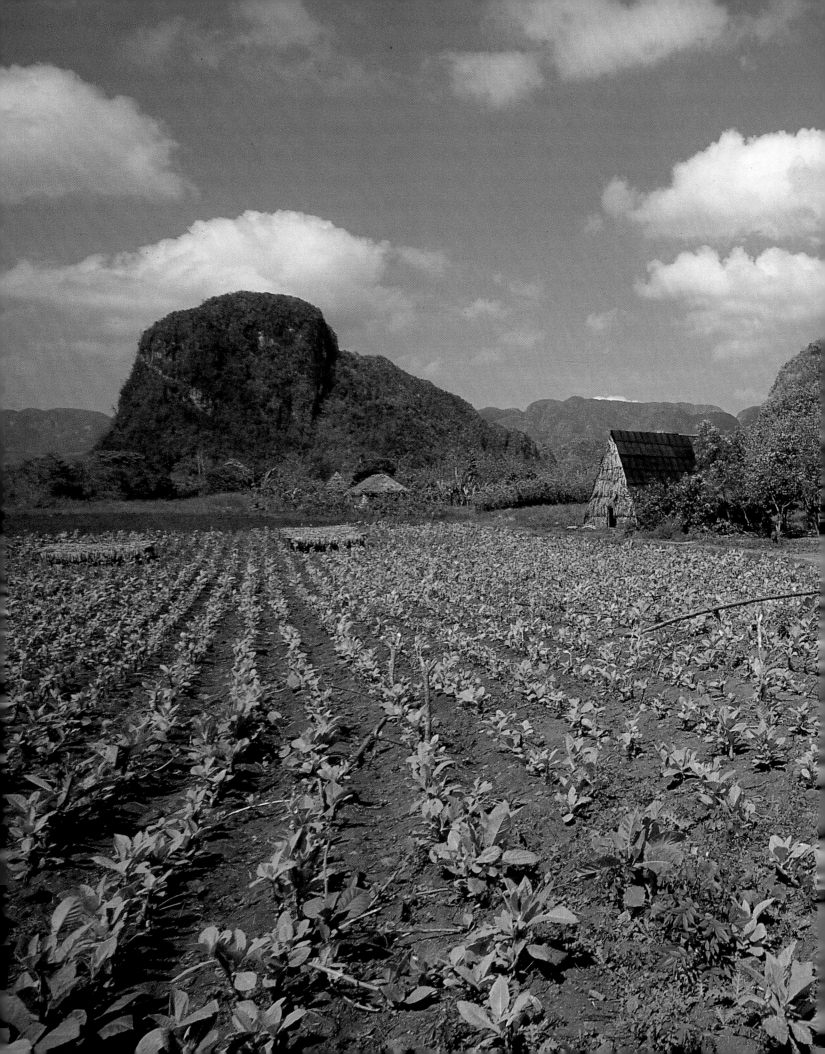

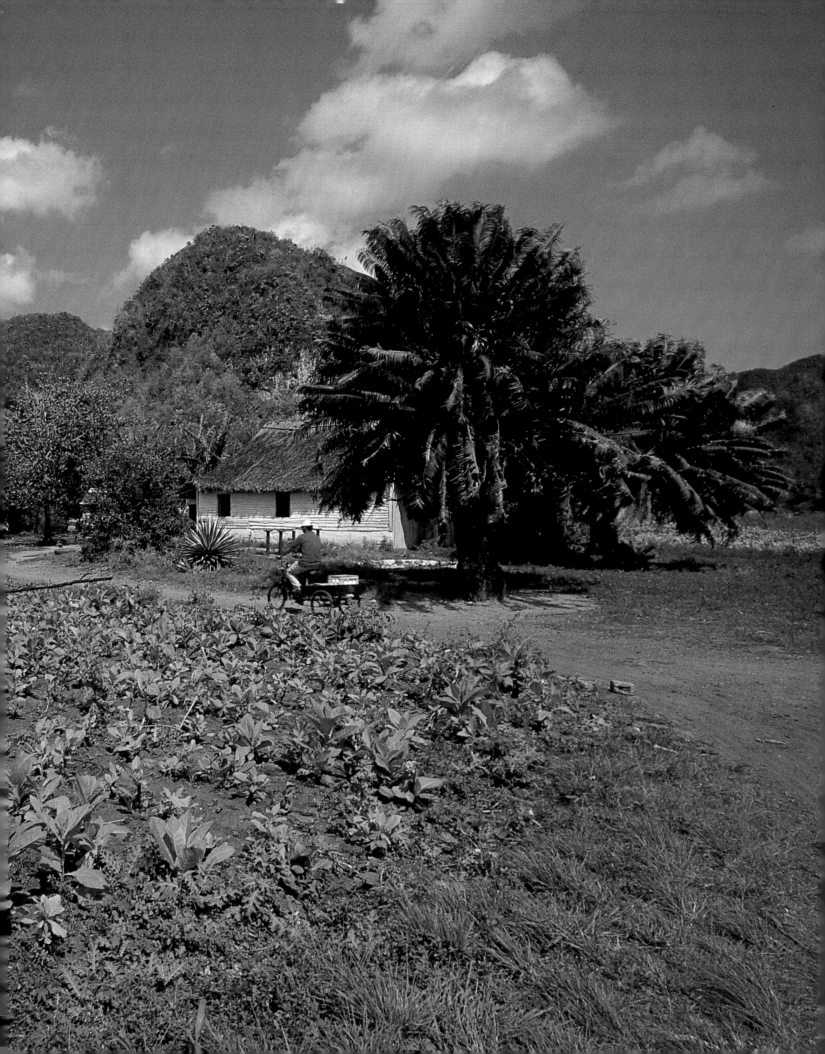

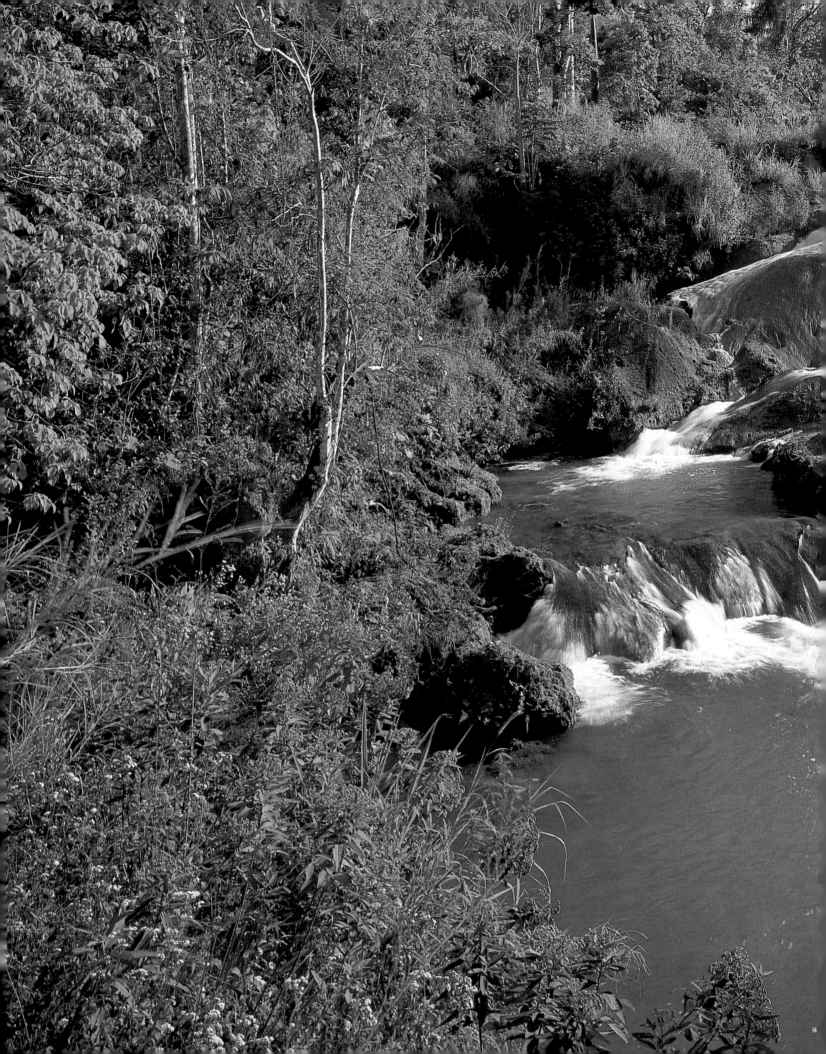

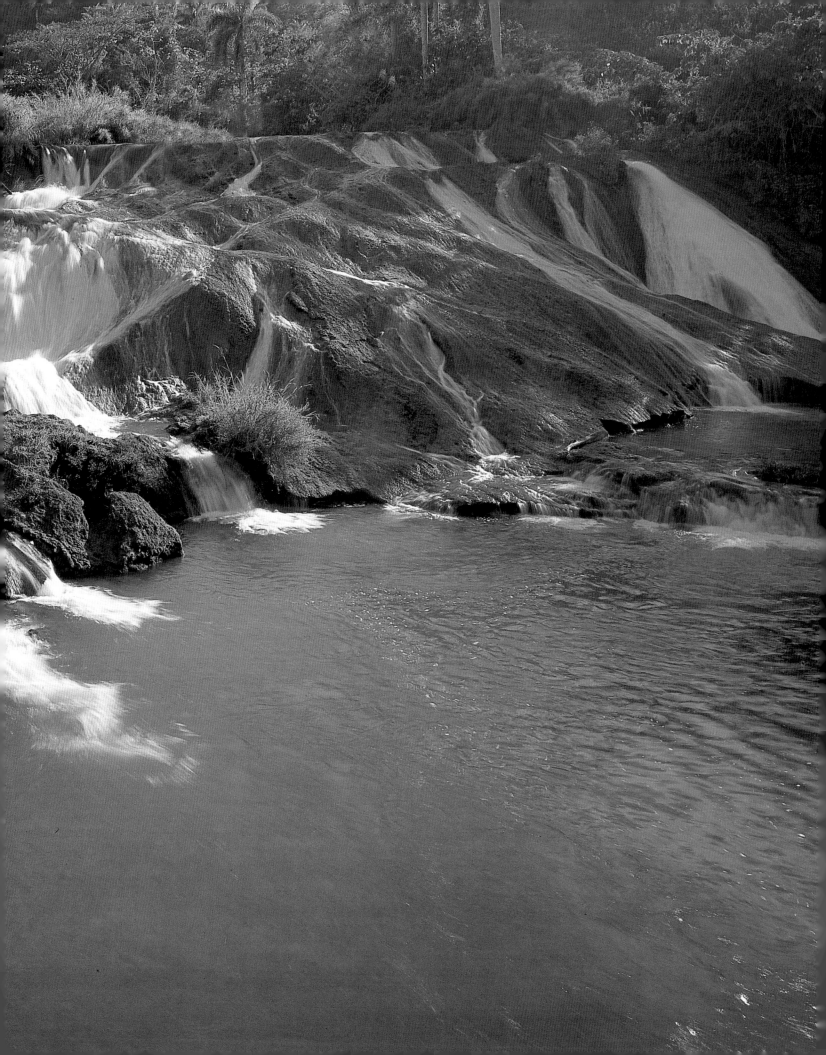

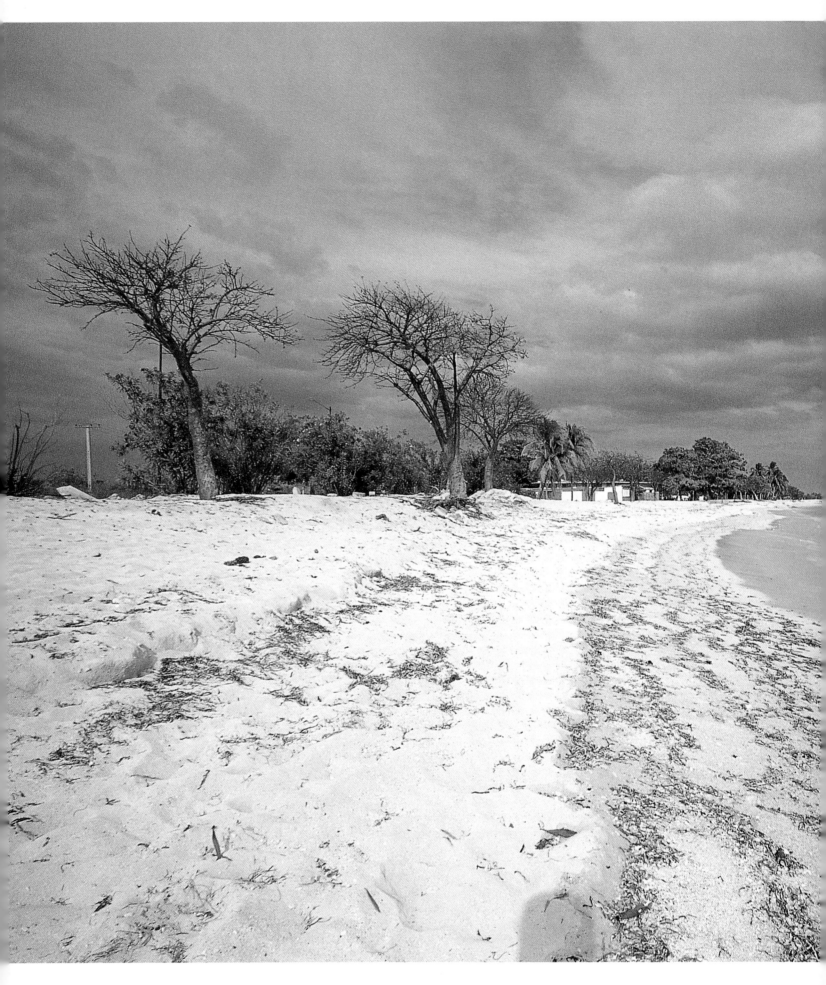

Gems of the Caribbean

54-55 and 55 Trinidad's beach, Playa Ancòn, is one of the loveliest on the island of Cuba and possibly better known than others. It also offers one of the most spectacular sights to be seen on the southern coast of Cuba: the sun rising over the Caribbean Sea. More hotels – in addition to the Soviet one built in the early '70s – have recently appeared along the coast of Playa Ancòn, now a popular tourist destination. Excursions to Cayo Blanco depart from the harbor of Casilda, close by.

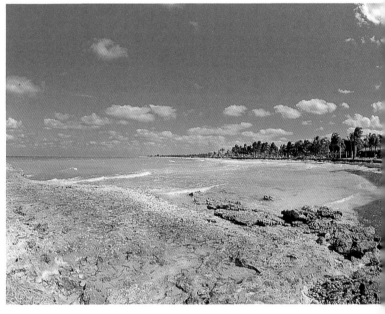

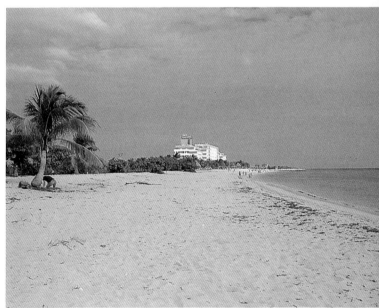

56 top and 56-57 *Playa de los Flamingos, on Cayo Coco, owes its name to the huge colony of pink flamingoes that inhabits several of the archipelago's islands. About 350 different species of birds live in Cuba, half of them using the island as a "stopover" during their annual migrations from north to south and vice versa. The island also boasts no fewer that 185 types of butterfly and over 1,000 different insects.*

56 bottom *An unexpected sight on Cayo Guillermo is the Hotel Flotante, built on a pontoon anchored in shallow water and looking not unlike a Mississippi paddle-steamer. It's a very simple structure but all its rooms have air conditioning and there are tiny balconies and verandas. All around, the blue-green water, fine warm sand and cloudless blue sky are more than enough to make guests feel blissfully at home in the world of the Tropics.*

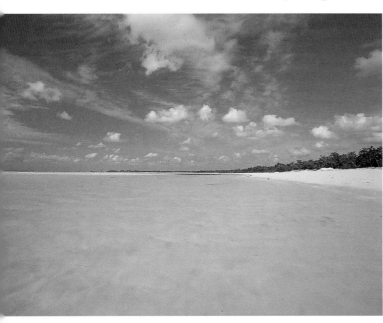

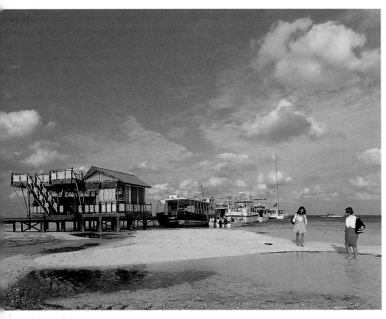

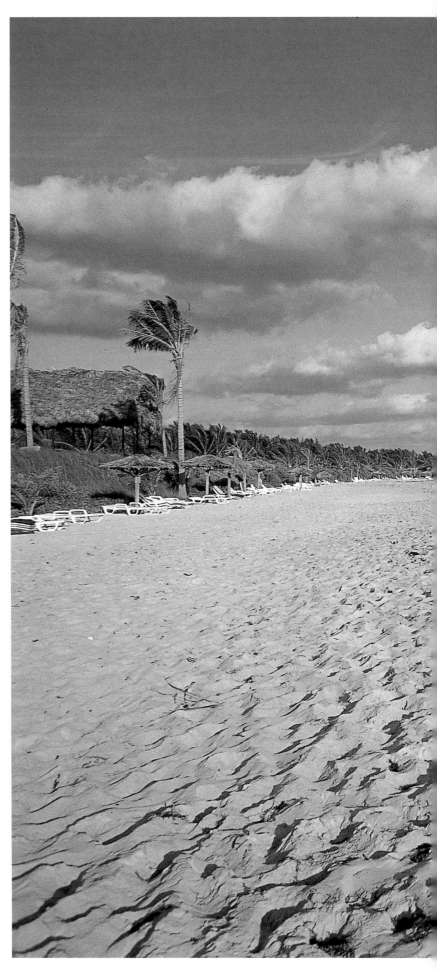

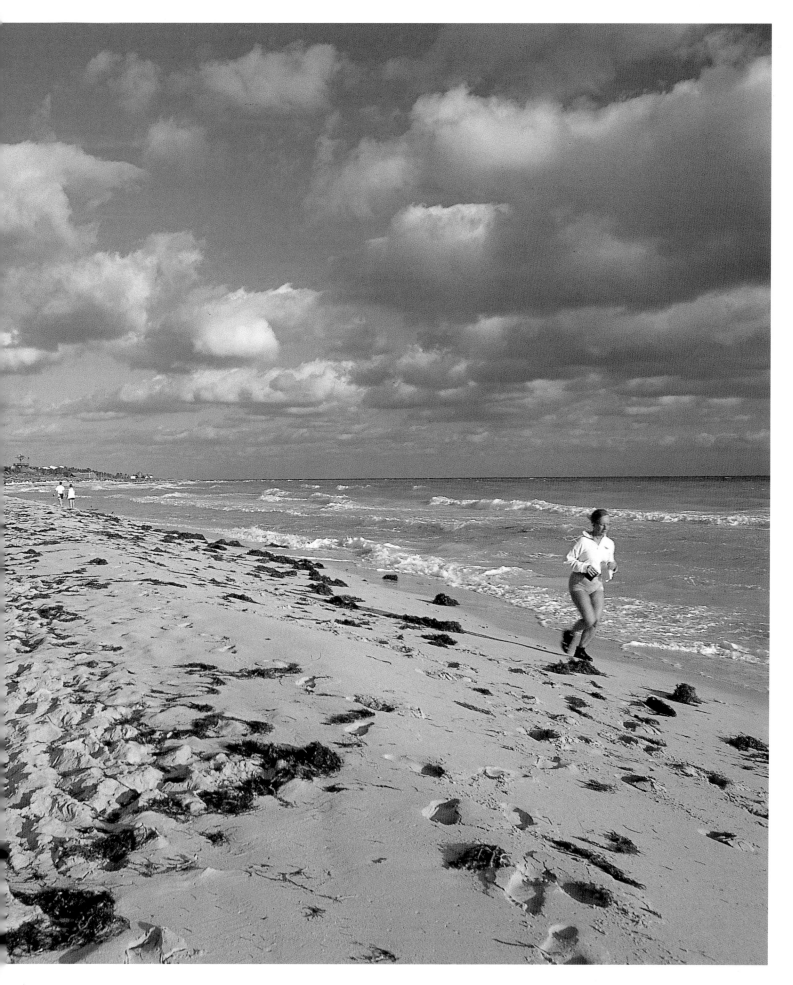

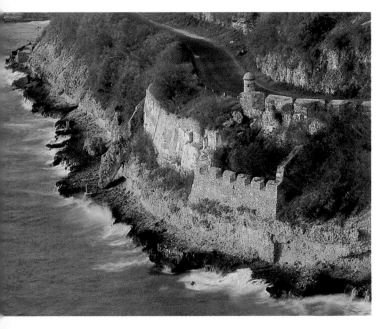

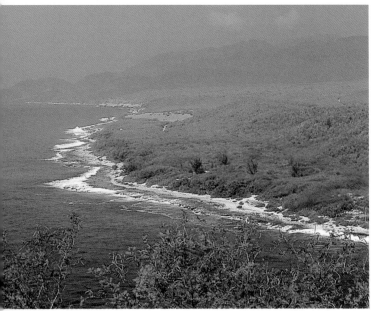

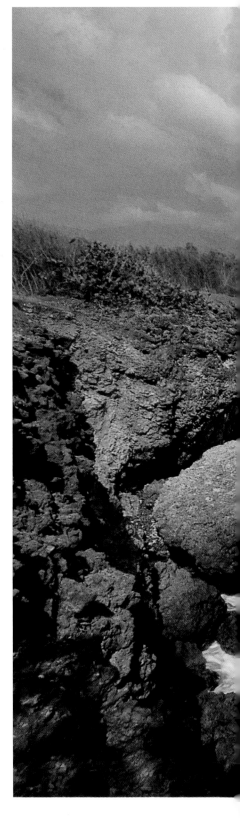

58 top *From the ramparts of the Castillo del Morro – a fortress built by the Spanish that now houses the Museum of Piracy – there is a fine view of Cayo Granma, only a short ferry trip away. Once used as a summer residence by well-heeled Santiagueros, it is now inhabited by fishermen and commuters. With neither cars nor hotels, the island enjoys the same peace and quiet as in days gone by.*

58 center *The bastions of the Castillo del Morro also afford a stunning view of the bay of Santiago. This fortress was designed by an Italian engineer named Antonelli, architect of the identical structure still standing in Havana. Since its completion in 1710 it has been used as a stronghold, barracks and prison. It was restored in 1978 and, within its labyrinthine passageways, staircases and drawbridges, now houses the Museum of Piracy.*

58 bottom *Cuba too has its prehistoric park, for the joy of both young and not-so-young. Visitors – in ever-increasing numbers since the success of the film Jurassic Park – seem to get immense pleasure and excitement from this opportunity for close encounters with the creatures who once populated the Earth. Parque Baconao is situated in the Valley of the Dinosaurs, about 31 miles southeast of Santiago.*

58-59 *Rocky shores are typical of the coastline around Santiago de Cuba, the island's most Caribbean city, where most of the population are blacks or mulattos and the atmosphere is reminiscent of the colonial era and life on the plantations. Thanks to its sheltered natural harbor on the coast of the Caribbean, Santiago was an important center of the slave trade that prospered on the island in the 17th and 18th centuries.*

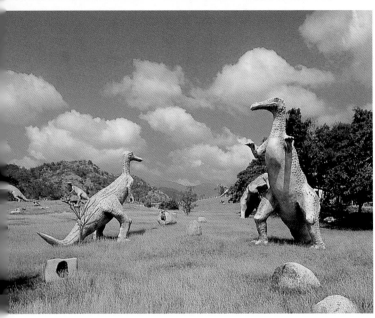

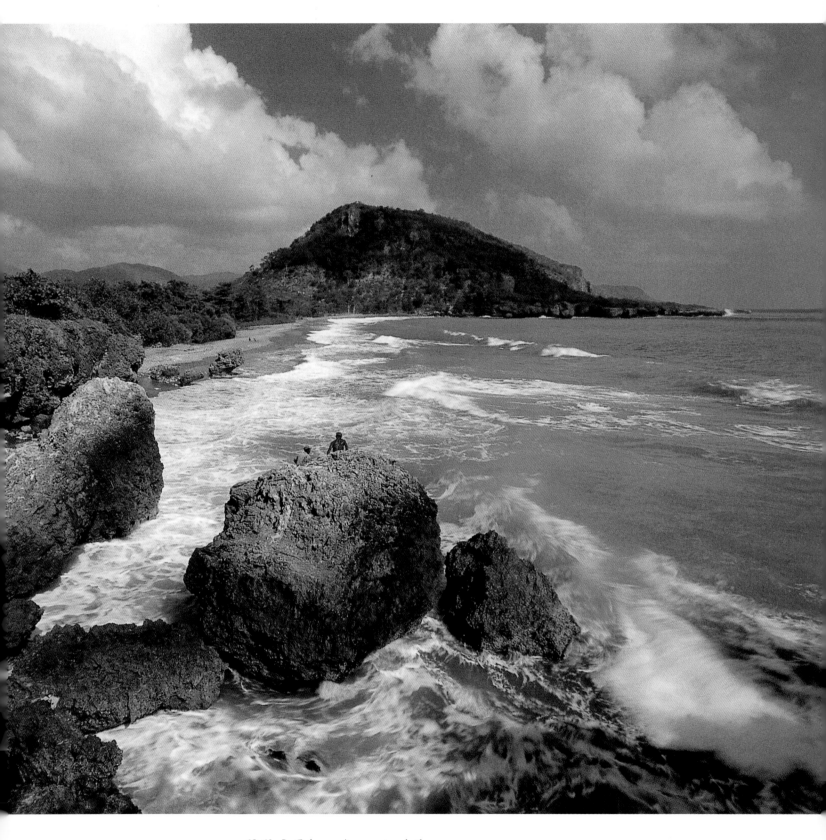

60-61 *In Cuba sunrise, sunset and other moments and atmospheric conditions can produce spectacular and phenomenonally beautiful sights. This photo – taken on the island of Cayo Guillermo in the archipelago of Camaguey – shows one such moment, when the sun seems about to set the sky ablaze with fiery shades of red and orange, only to fade slowly as dusk approaches.*

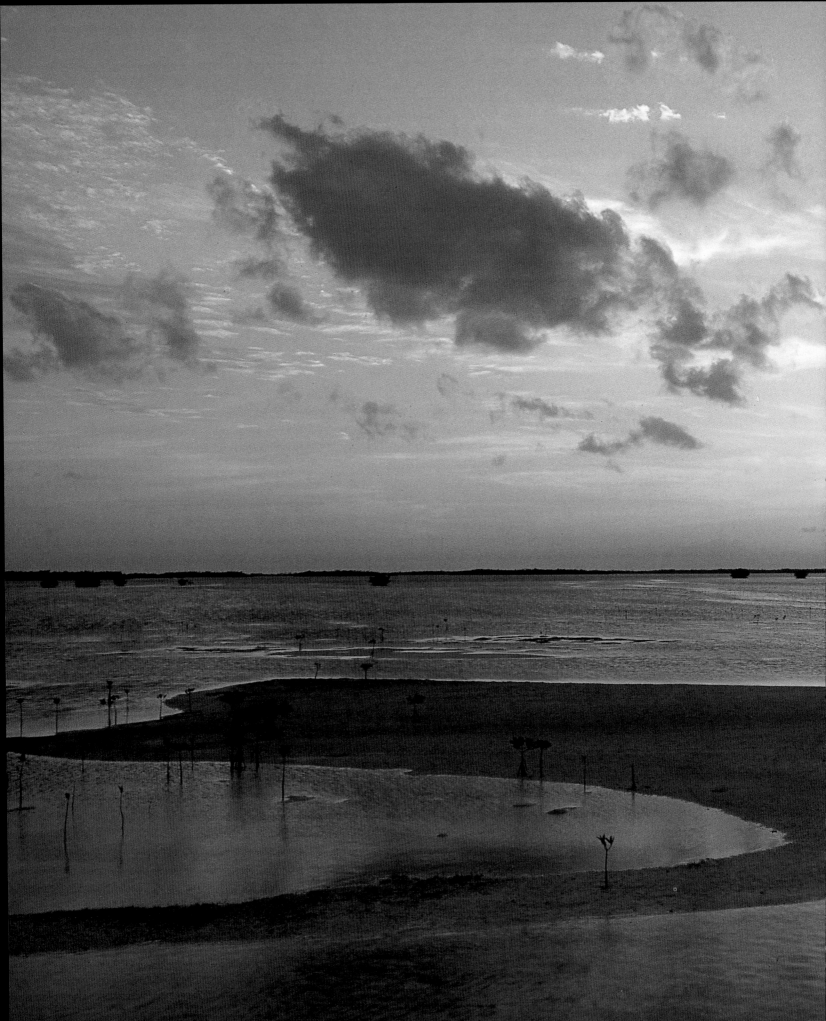

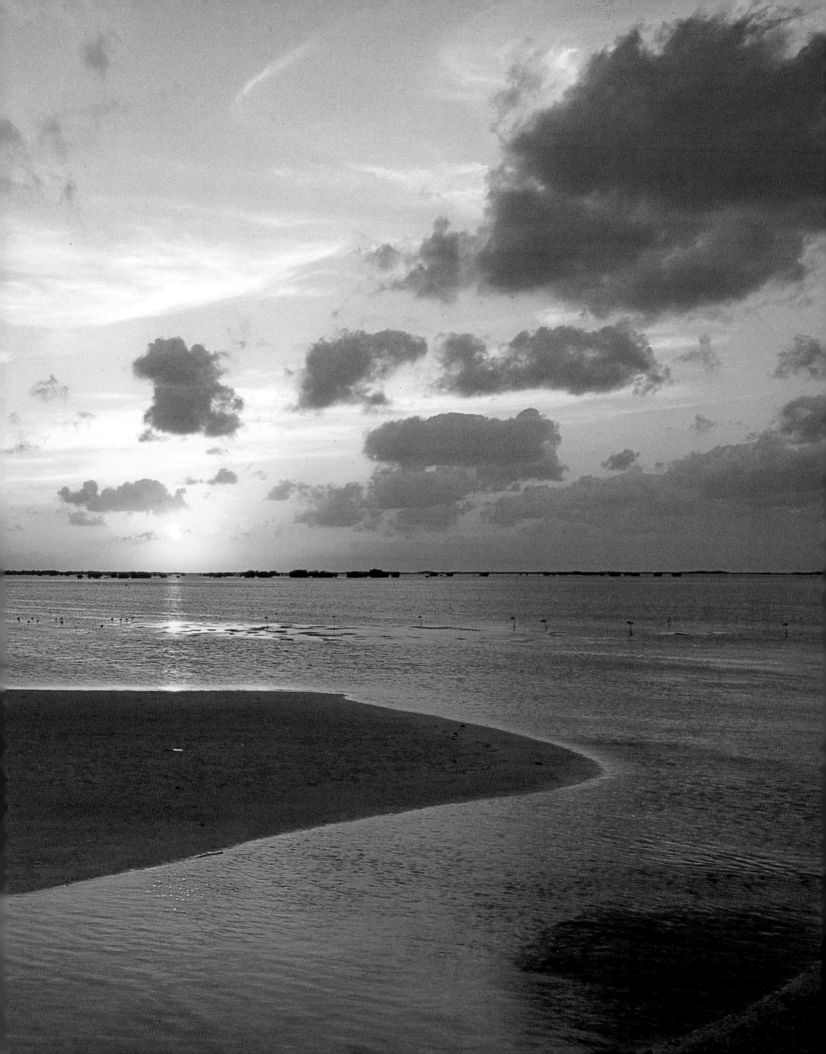

Splendid testimonies of the colonial era

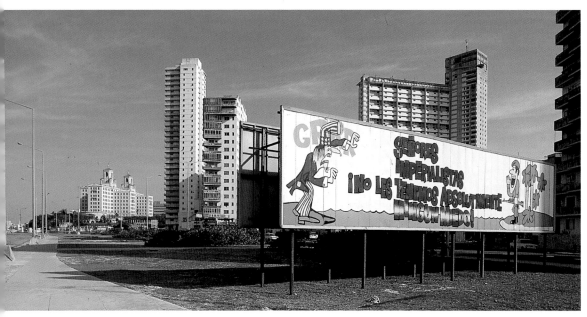

62 top *The modern face of Havana's Vedado district is much in evidence, especially from the Malecòn, the six-lane promenade that extends for 3 miles along the seafront and is always crowded with pedlars, families and young couples. All along the streets are huge and somewhat simplistic posters that pour scorn on imperialist America and extol the values of the Castrist Revolution.*

62 bottom *The Casa de la Cultura in Cienfuegos, Cuba's second most important industrial center and capital of the province of the same name. The city is of fairly recent origin (1819). After the 1959 Revolution, huge sums were invested here by the Soviet Union and Cienfuegos became a major center of industry, with towering silos, cement and chemical fertilizer plants, mills and shipyards.*

63 *Santa Clara, capital of Villa Clara province, was founded in 1690 in the region's interior by families fleeing repeated pirate attacks on the coastal town of San Juan de Los Remedios. Among the late 19th-century buildings that overlook the tree-lined Parque Vidal, the main square, is the Hotel Santa Clara Libre: it still bears evidence of the battle fought here by Che Guevara in 1958.*

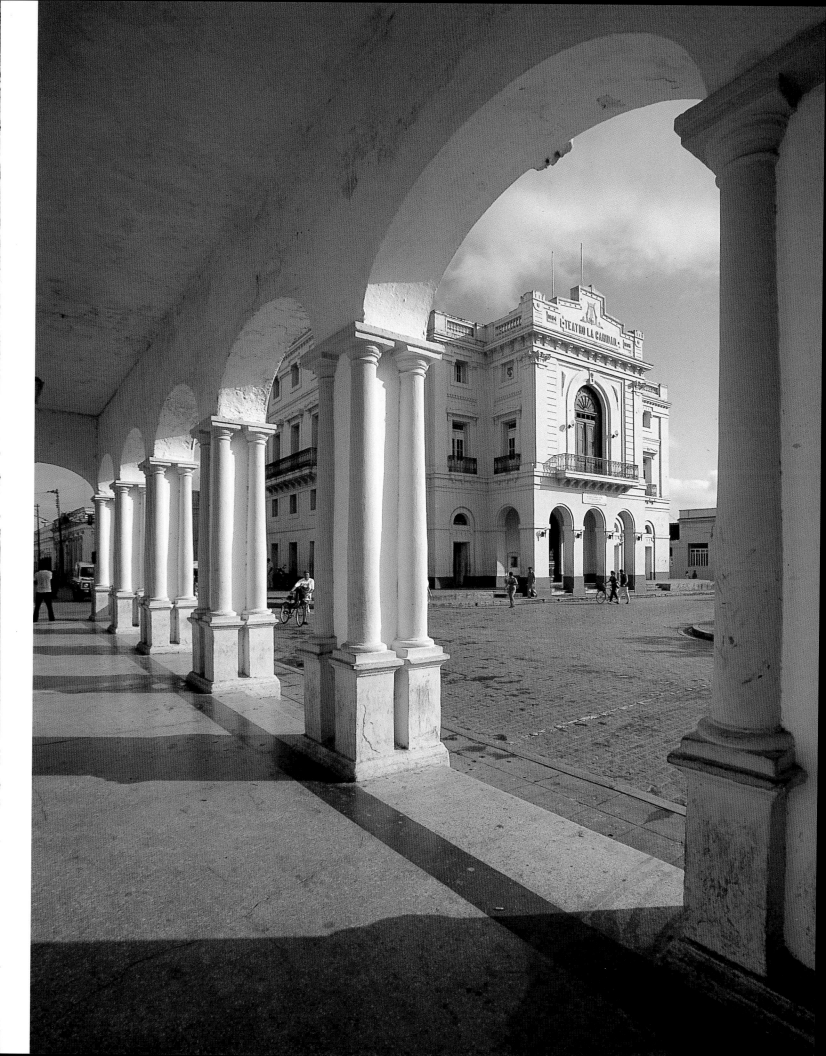

Havana, decrepit queen of the Caribbean

64 top left *Beside the Capitolio Nacional, on the open Parque Central, is the García Lorca – ex Nacional – Theater. It was built in 1838, in an eclectic style, and was subsequently dedicated to the Spanish poet assassinated during the Civil War.*

64 bottom left *A close-up of the exterior of the García Lorca Theater, on the Parque Central in Havana. It has more than one auditorium: the ballet company practices in rooms overlooking the street while drama productions are rehearsed in those at the rear.*

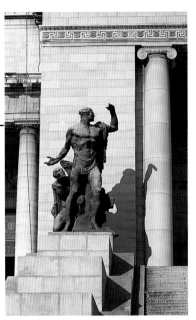

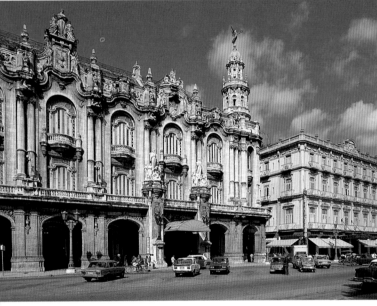

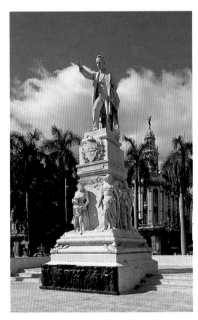

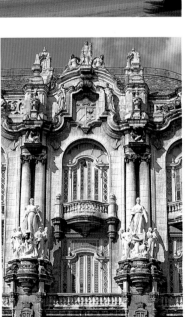

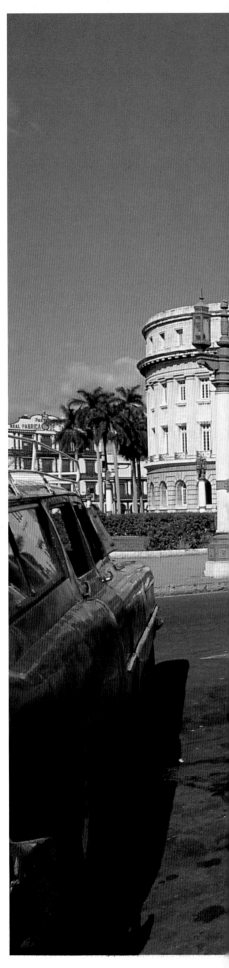

64 top right *Abundant marble, sweeping staircases, tall pillars and imposing statues: all adding up to a solemn statement fitting for the Capitolio Nacional, a precise copy of the Capitol in Washington D.C.*

64 bottom right *In every Cuban village and in many cities of Latin America too, an effigy, bust or statue of José Martí adorns the main square. In Havana the statue of the man who founded Cuba's Revolutionary Party stands in the middle of the Parque Central.*

64-65 *Offering a colorful contrast to Havana's Capitolio Nacional are bright American cars, survivors from the '50s. The building was the seat of the Càmara de Rapresentants for 30 years. It now houses the Academia de Ciencias de Cuba and the Museo de Ciencias Naturales.*

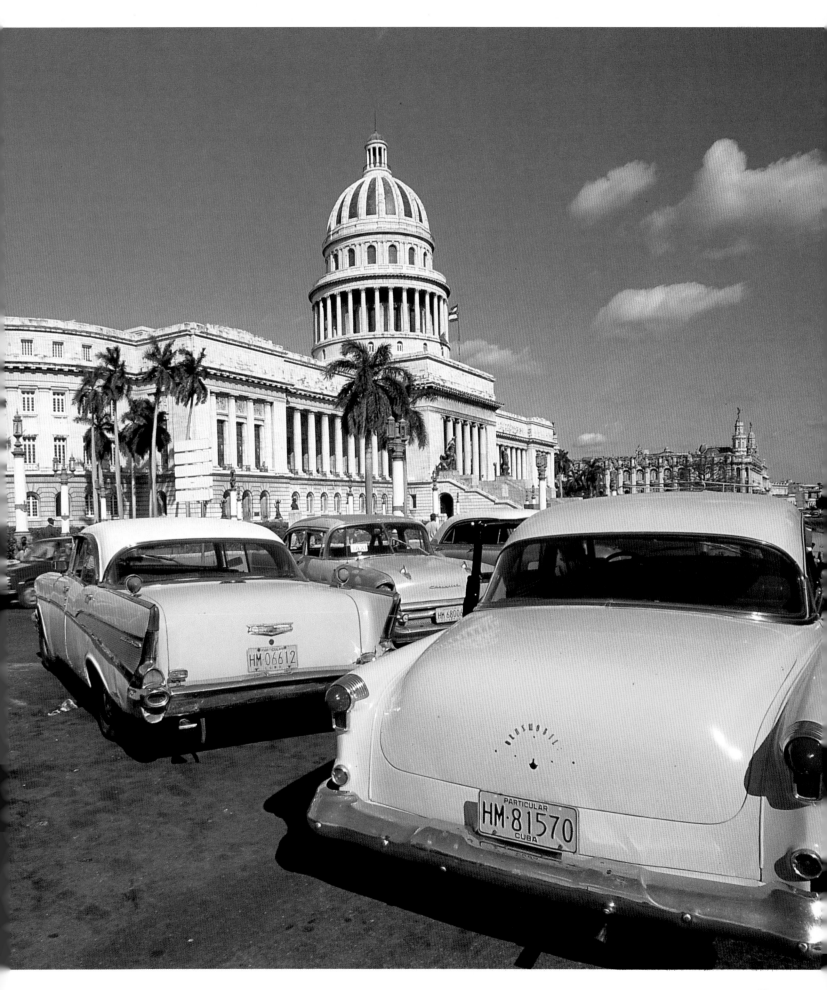

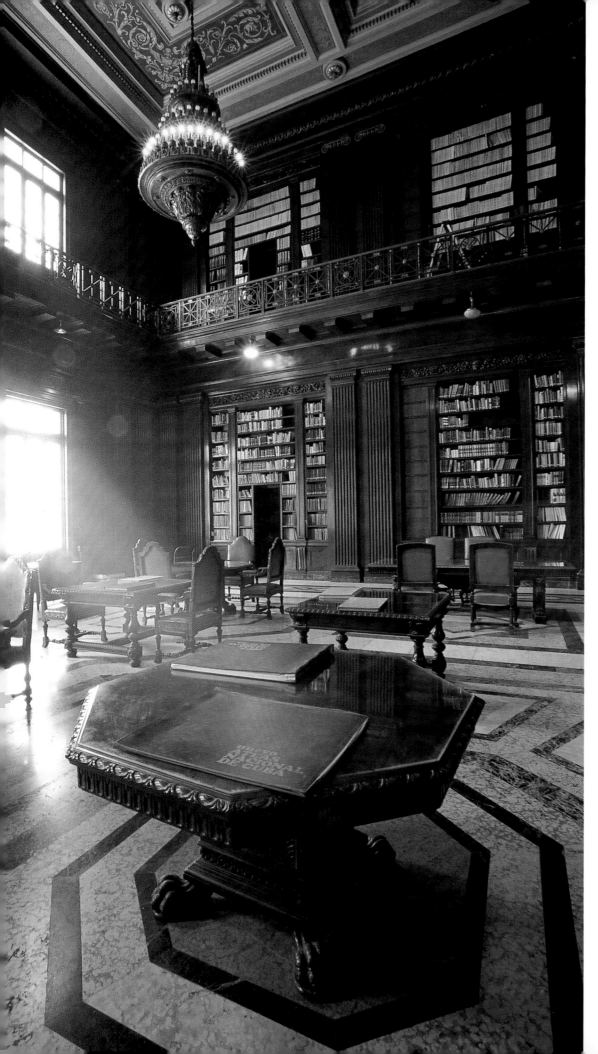

66 left *The many technical books comprising the library named after José Martí cover the walls of a huge room in the Capitolio Nacional.*
The room is beautifully decorated and furnished: inlaid floors featuring marble of different colors and provenance, antique furniture and a magnificent chandelier.

66 right *The Salòn de los Escudos in Havana's Capitolio Nacional is in Renaissance style, with coffered ceiling, doors made from finest-quality wood. This room was used for official dinners when Gerardo Machado and Fulgencio Batista were in power, and the tables are still laid and decorated to show how they once looked when in use.*

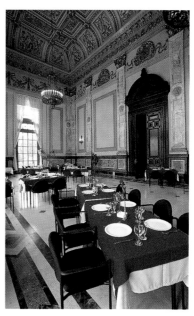

67 left *The magnificent "Hall of Lost Steps" in the Capitolio Nacional is in Italian Renaissance style, with a barrel ceiling and a row of windows running along each side. The floor of inlaid marble is classical in design.*

67 right *Another of the richly adorned official rooms in the Capitolio Nacional in Havana, which is a copy of the Capitol in Washington, USA, is the Round Room, beneath the gigantic dome.*

68-69 *The bar on the 25th floor of the famous Habana Libre Hotel affords a wonderful view over the whole city, as far as the outskirts. In this photo the Malecòn (the seafront promenade) can just be seen in the distance while on the left is the white Hotel Nacional with its twin towers and a lot of retro charm.*

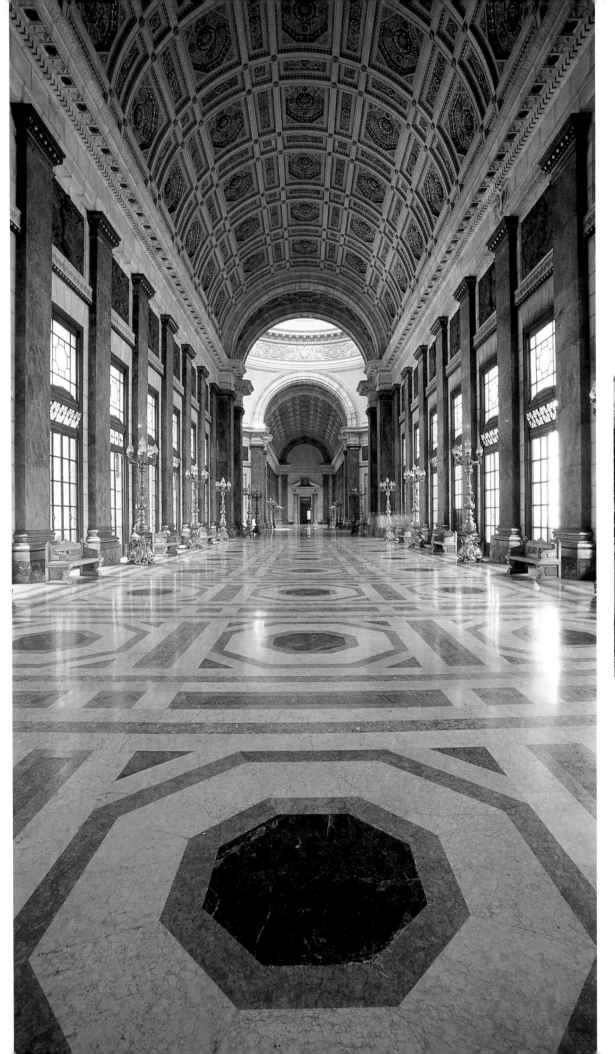

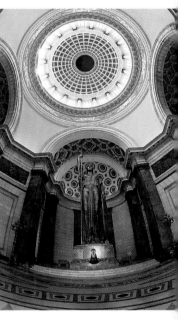

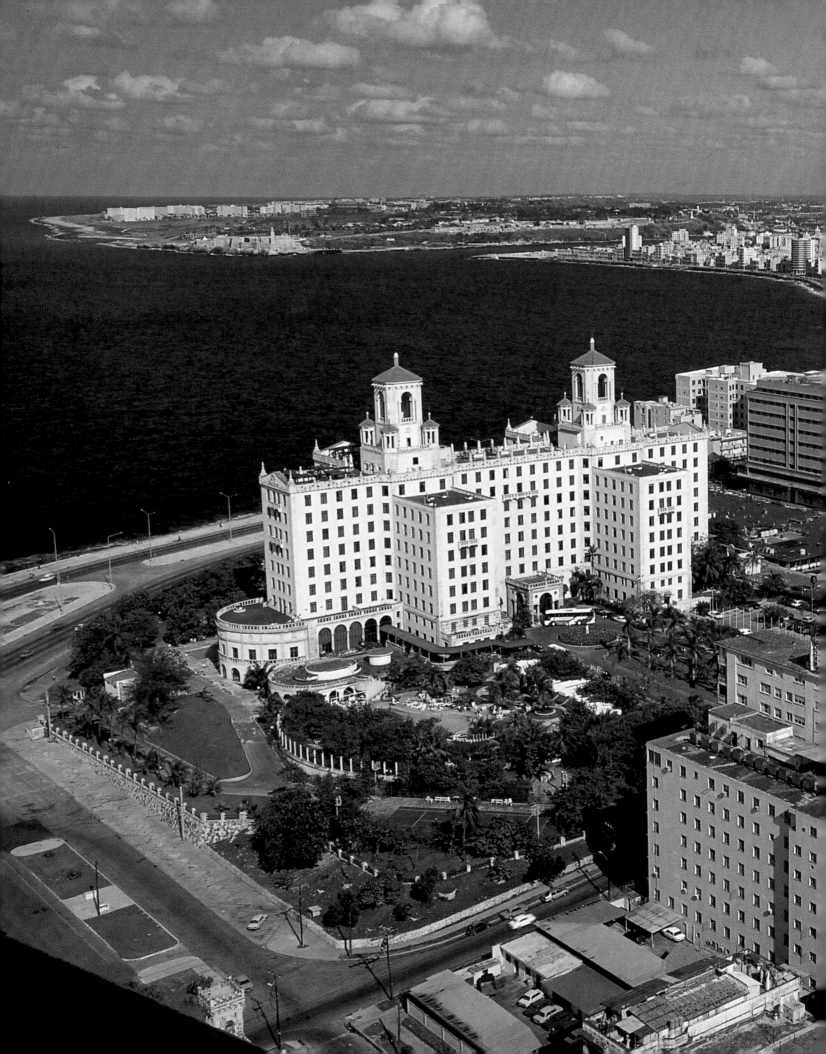

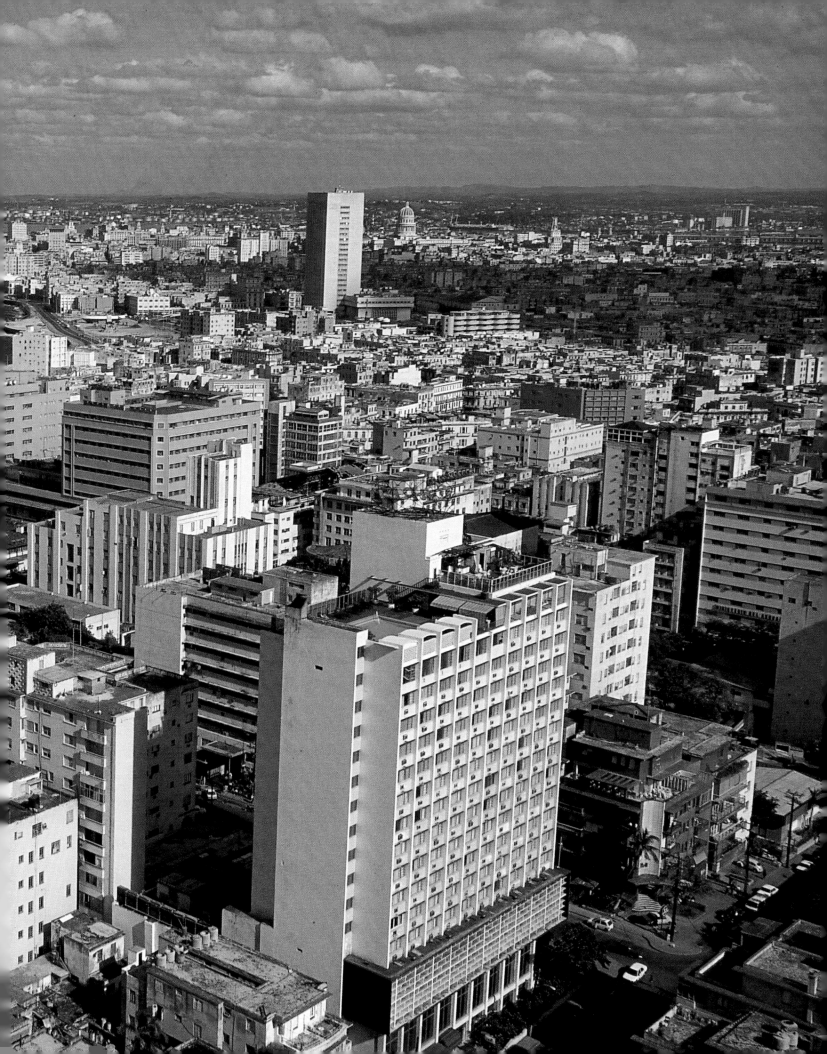

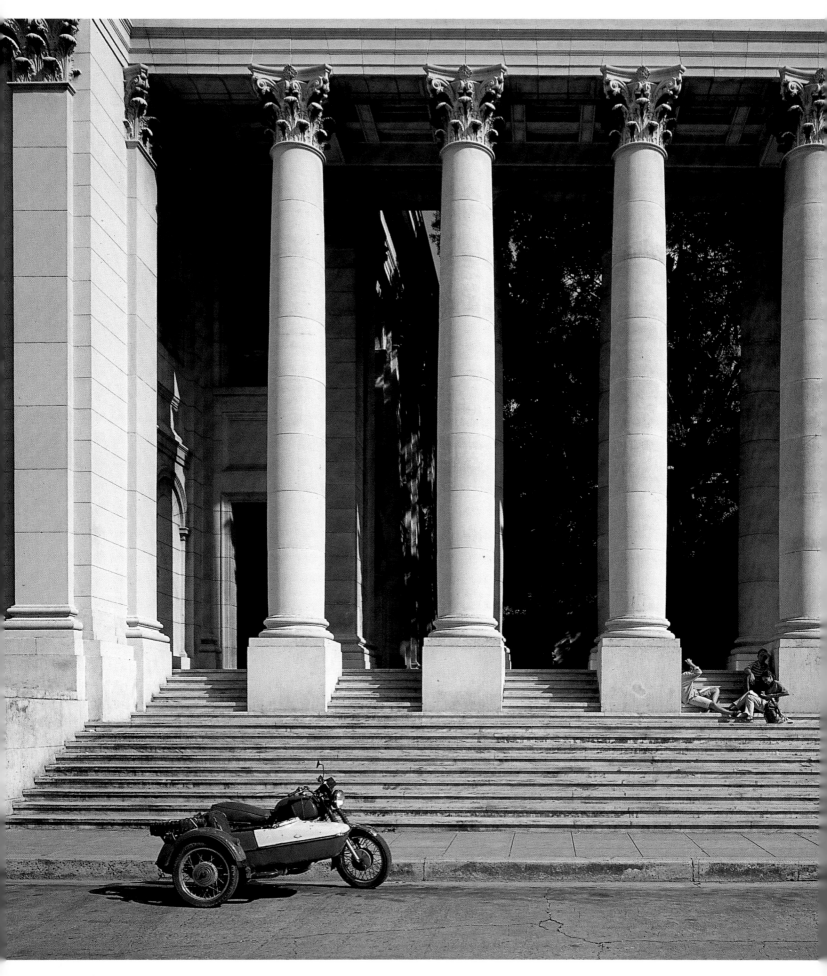

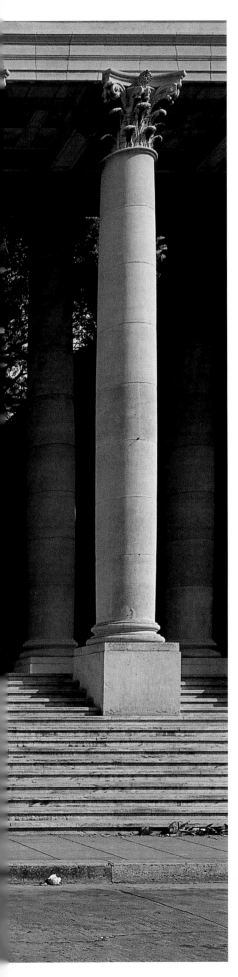

70-71 *Tall, slender columns are a characterizing feature of the neoclassical façade of the main building of the University of Havana, which occupies a large area in the city's Vedado district. Education for all has been one of the main goals of the Castrist regime since its very earliest days. Now 95% of the island's population has attended school and in this respect Cuba leads the world, among industrialized as well as developing nations.*

71 bottom right *One of Havana's best known hotels is the Habana Riviera. First opened in 1950, it still has the look of a luxury hotel of those days but its facilities are modern and of a high standard. The restaurant is renowned for its Creole cuisine. Located close to the Malecón, it offers superb views over Havana and the coast. It is part of the Gran Caribe hotel chain, famous throughout the Antilles.*

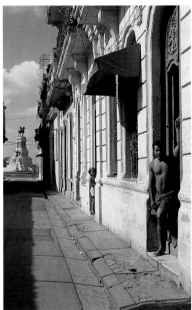

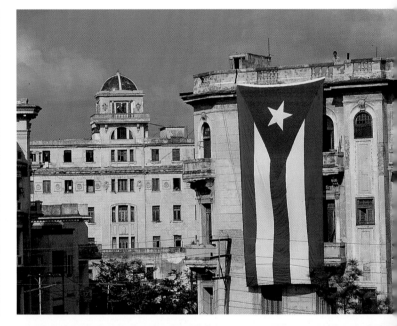

71 left *Many buildings and quarters of Havana retain their fine architectural features but are clearly suffering from neglect. Although it still exudes the charm of the great Spanish city, Habana Vieja shows signs of the economic crisis caused by the collapse of the Soviet bloc. A recent series of reforms has nonetheless opened the door to both foreign investments and some forms of free enterprise.*

71 top right *The national flag flutters from a rooftop in Havana. The Cuban flag was designed by Miguel Teurba Tolòn in 1849. Its white stripes represent peace, the blue ones the three provinces into which the island was once divided. The red triangle recalls the blood shed in the struggle for independence from Spain. The white five-pointed star symbolizes the freedom won by the Cuban people after centuries-long domination.*

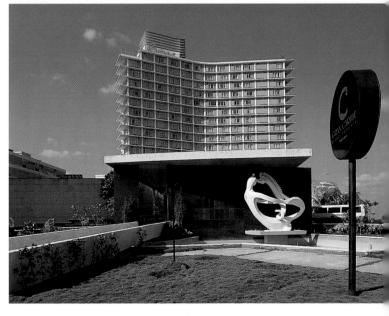

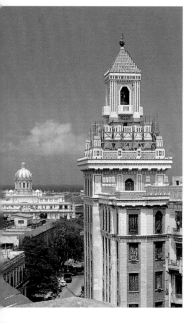

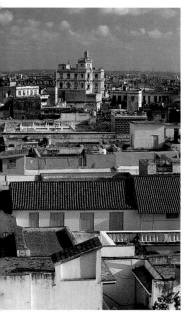

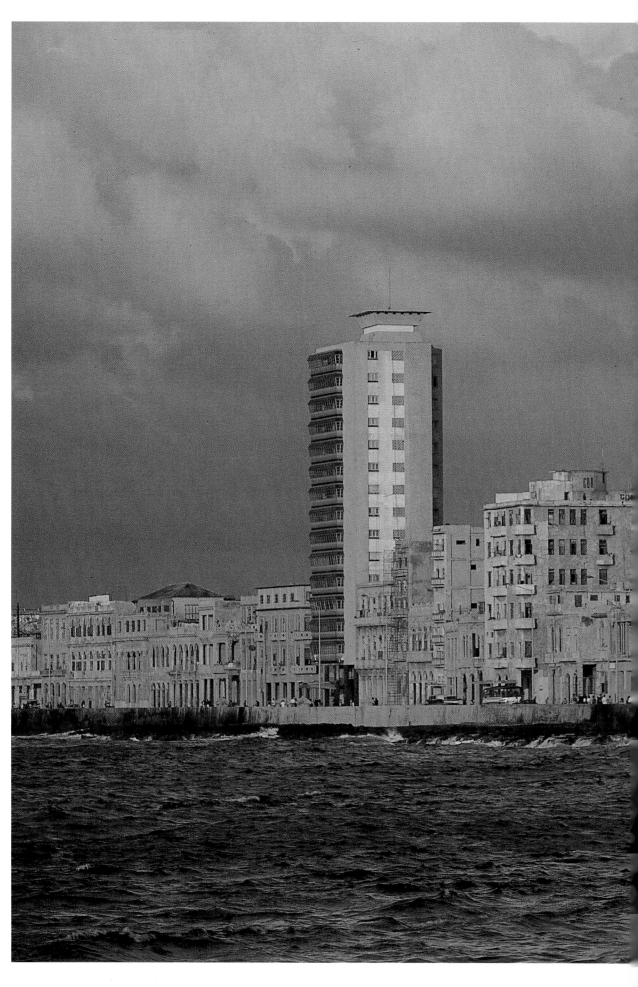

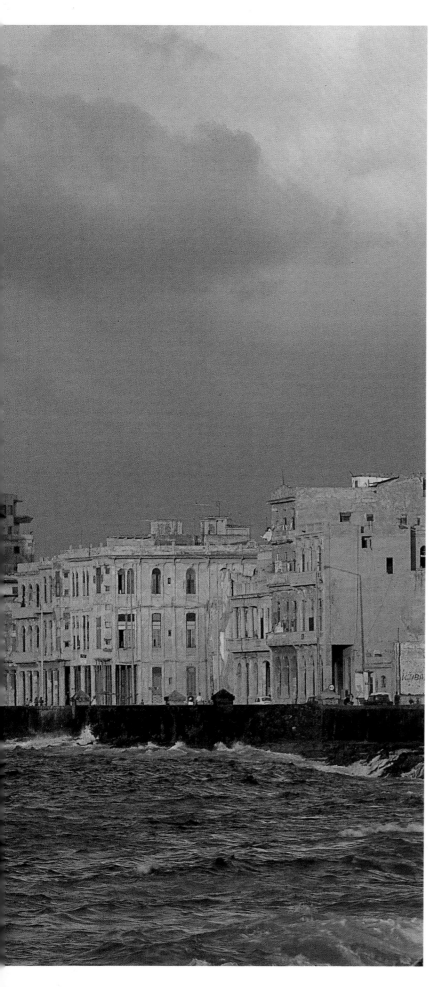

72 top *The Bacardi Building, once home of the Bacardi Rum Company, is an ostentatious structure of eclectic design close to the Floridita restaurant, between Via Progreso and Via Monserrate. At street level it's difficult to see the whole of the building, especially the upper floors where there is a statue of a huge bat. The ideal vantage point is the top floor of the Plaza Hotel, directly opposite.*

72 bottom *Houses in the old parts of Havana are generally low, with red-tiled roofs in the old Spanish style; their walls are often painted in pastel colors like yellow, pink, pale blue and light green. Habana Vieja is the largest colonial settlement remaining in Latin America. A conservation scheme, introduced in the '70s, received a significant boost from funds allocated by UNESCO.*

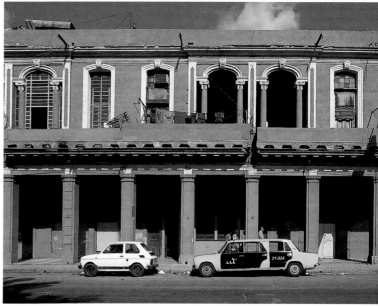

72-73 *Seen here from a distance, the Malecón, Havana's broad seafront promenade, starts from the Castillo de la Punta and runs along the ocean towards La Rampa, past the Hotel Nacional and Hotel Riviera. It ends at the mouth of the Río Almendares, which divides the Vedado district from Miramar. An air of nostalgia hangs over the Malecón; the pastel colors of its buildings are now faded by time and the salty sea air.*

73 *This typical house in the old city center – painted blue, with a ground floor portico and arched windows on the first floor – recalls Spain, and especially Andalusia. More and more buildings like this one, very common in Havana, are being restored, and appreciable results will be seen in a few years' time.*

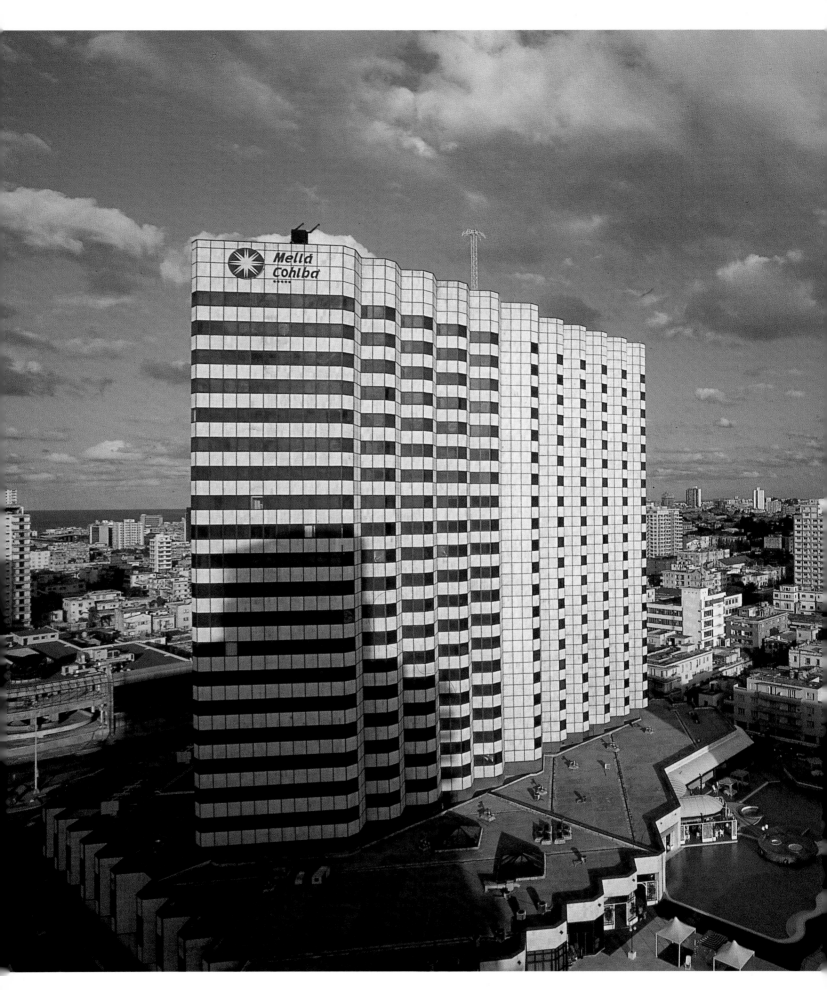

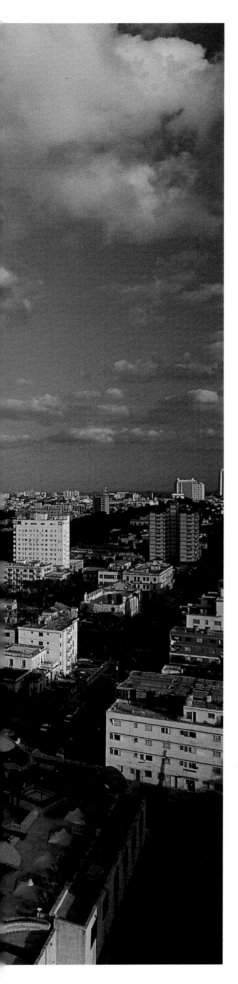

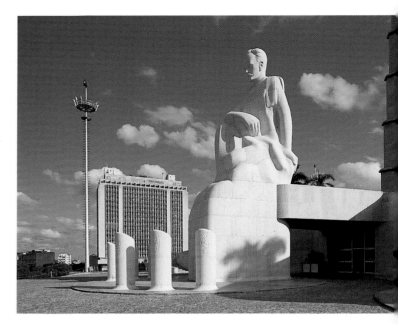

74-75 *Urban development in Havana has been characterized by stops and starts. The end of Batista's dictatorship interrupted his plan to demolish and rebuild Habana Vieja. The revolutionary government has made some progress with improvement schemes and restoration but has also encouraged projects for contemporary structures like this hotel, the Melìa Cohiba, on Avenida Paseo.*

75 top *This much debated and criticized monument in white marble, dedicated to the national hero, José Martí, stands in Plaza de la Revolución beside a 473-foot obelisk. Although work on the huge column began under Batista, it was completed only after his downfall and in fact soon became a symbol of the Revolution. Huge political rallies celebrating important events in the history of Castrist Cuba take place in this vast open space.*

75 center *To enter the port of Havana, ships have to pass through a bottleneck channel. Guarding this strait on one side, at the start of the Malecón, is the Castillo de San Salvador de la Punta; on the other side, in Habana del Este, is the Castillo del Morro. A nearby tunnel allows road traffic to cross the strait without having to use the ferry.*

75 bottom *Plaza de la Revolución, with its obelisk and monument to José Martí, is situated to the south of the hotels district. Various ministry buildings line its sides: the one occupied by the Ministry of the Interior most often appears in photos on account of its famous portrait of Che Guevara, with the words "Hasta la victoria siempre". The other buildings overlooking the plaza – such as the Ministry of Justice where the Central Committee of the Communist Party meets and Castro himself has his office – are grey and anonymous.*

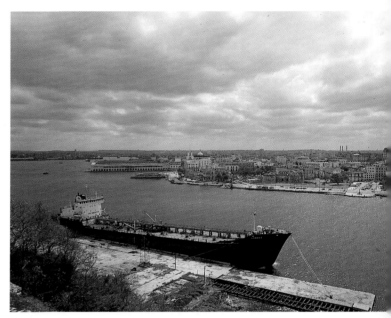

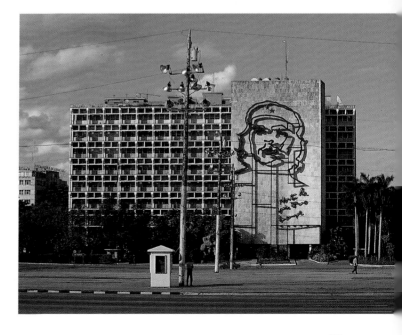

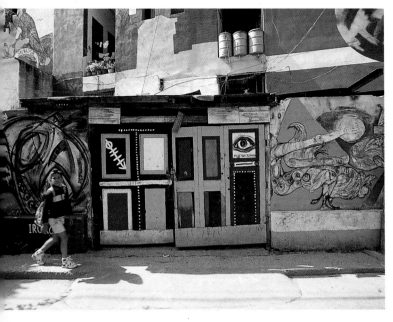

76 top left *It is not unusual to find reminders of Cuba's African origins in the impromptu paintings that decorate houses in Havana, as in this photo taken in Calle Jon de Jamel, where symbols like fishbones and eyes emerge from squares of darker colors. More formalized art often favors abstract designs too and Afro-Cuban mythology and folklore figure large in the work of the younger generation of artists.*

76 center left *With the gradual introduction of "free trade", at an individual level at least, much of Habana Vieja has turned into a kind of Cuban souq, with stalls selling anything and everything. Plaza des Armas, the oldest square in the city, is once again thronged with crowds drawn by a market where pictures, posters and old books are the main attraction.*

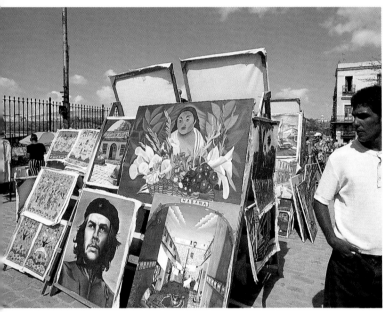

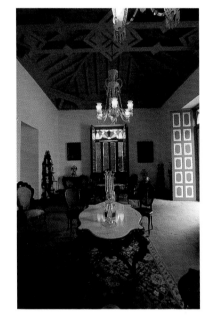

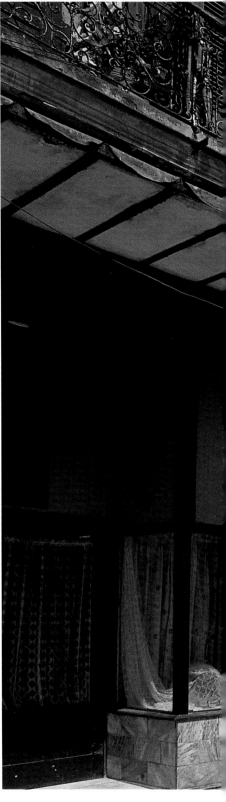

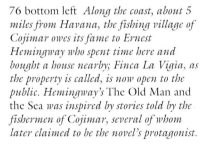

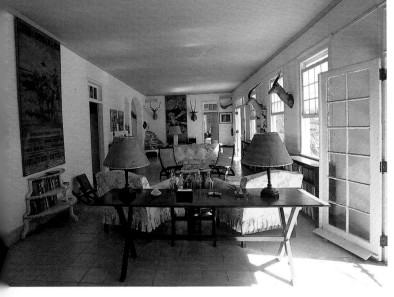

76 bottom left *Along the coast, about 5 miles from Havana, the fishing village of Cojimar owes its fame to Ernest Hemingway who spent time here and bought a house nearby; Finca La Vigìa, as the property is called, is now open to the public. Hemingway's* The Old Man and the Sea *was inspired by stories told by the fishermen of Cojimar, several of whom later claimed to be the novel's protagonist.*

76 right *Testimonies to a fascinating chapter in Cuba's history are displayed in the Museo de Arte Colonial. The museum is housed in the Palacio de los Condes de Casa Bayona, in Calle San Ignacio, facing Plaza de la Catedral. Its vast collections of furnishings, chandeliers, glasswares and ceramics come from the splendid homes of Havana's former colonial aristocracy and cover the period from the 17th to 19th centuries.*

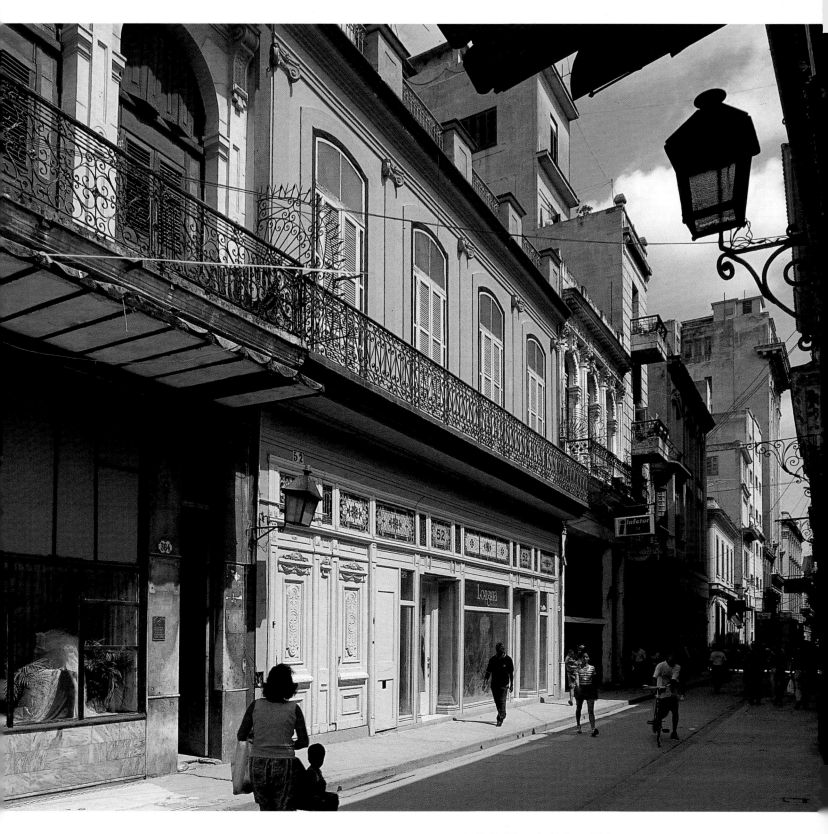

76-77 *Calle Obispo, in Habana Vieja, is part of the classic route followed by Hemingway devotees and rum fanciers because right here, at no. 557, is the Floridita, the bar where the writer passed his time sipping daiquiris. Many of the old houses with balconies along the street have been restructured and painted in the traditional pale shades of blue, pink, green and yellow.*

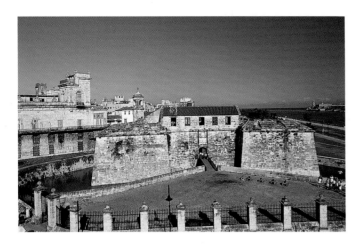

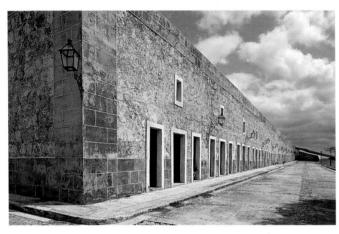

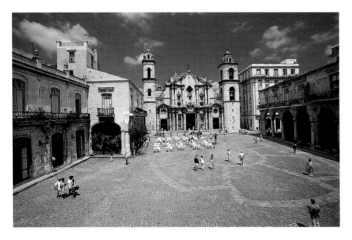

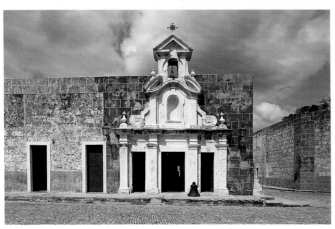

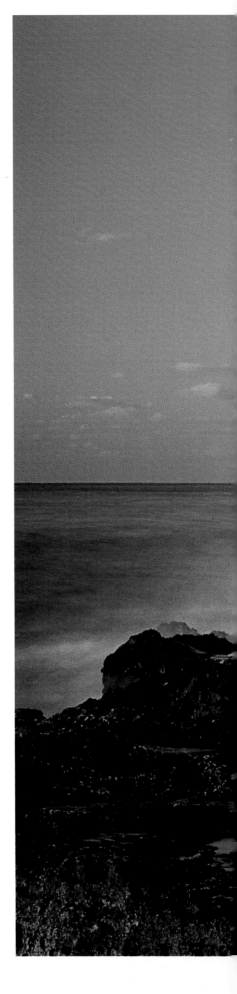

78 top *The courtyard of the Castillo de le Fuerza viewed from the bastions, looking towards the bottleneck channel at the entrance to the harbor. Visible in the distance is the Castillo del Moro, constructed with rocks from nearby shores. The Castillo de la Fuerza is the oldest fortress in the Americas. Built between 1558 and 1634 it was also the residence of the governor and Captains of the Spanish Crown who ruled the colony.*

78 top center *The sinister-looking Fortaleza de San Carlos de la Cabana was built between 1764 and 1774, work having started immediately after the end of British occupation of Havana. In the centuries that followed, it never played a defensive role; it was a prison during the period of dictatorship that ended with the Castrist revolution. Now restored, it houses the Military Academy.*

78 bottom center *Plaza de la Catedral is a very fine example of colonial baroque architecture. Construction of the cathedral started in the early 1700s and was completed only at the end of the century. The influence of Italian baroque is evident in the façade. The bells of the two bell-towers are known affectionately as San Pedro and San Miguel.*

78 bottom *A small church whose architecture combines late baroque with neoclassical elements is part of the monumental complex of the Fortaleza de la Cabana, built on a hill on the east side of Havana, overlooking the entrance to the harbor.*

78-79 *From Habana Vieja the Tunnel della Bahìa passes beneath the strait at the mouth of the harbor, at a depth of 40 feet below sea level. It leads to the Castillo de Los Tres Reyes del Morro, a fortress with a distinctive irregular polygonal shape, built between 1589 and 1610 to a project by Battista Antonelli. A feature of particular interest is the legendary battery of 12 cannons bearing the names of the 12 apostles. In 1762 the fortress withstood a 44-day seige by the British fleet.*

80-81 *Seen from the mouth of the strait leading into the harbor, the Malecón reveals the full force of its untamed beauty, as ocean rollers break against its edge. Along the promenade, which continues all the way to Vedado, is the monument recalling the explosion abroad the USS "Maine" in Havana harbor on February 19th 1898. The incident was used by Washington as a pretext for declaring war on Spain.*

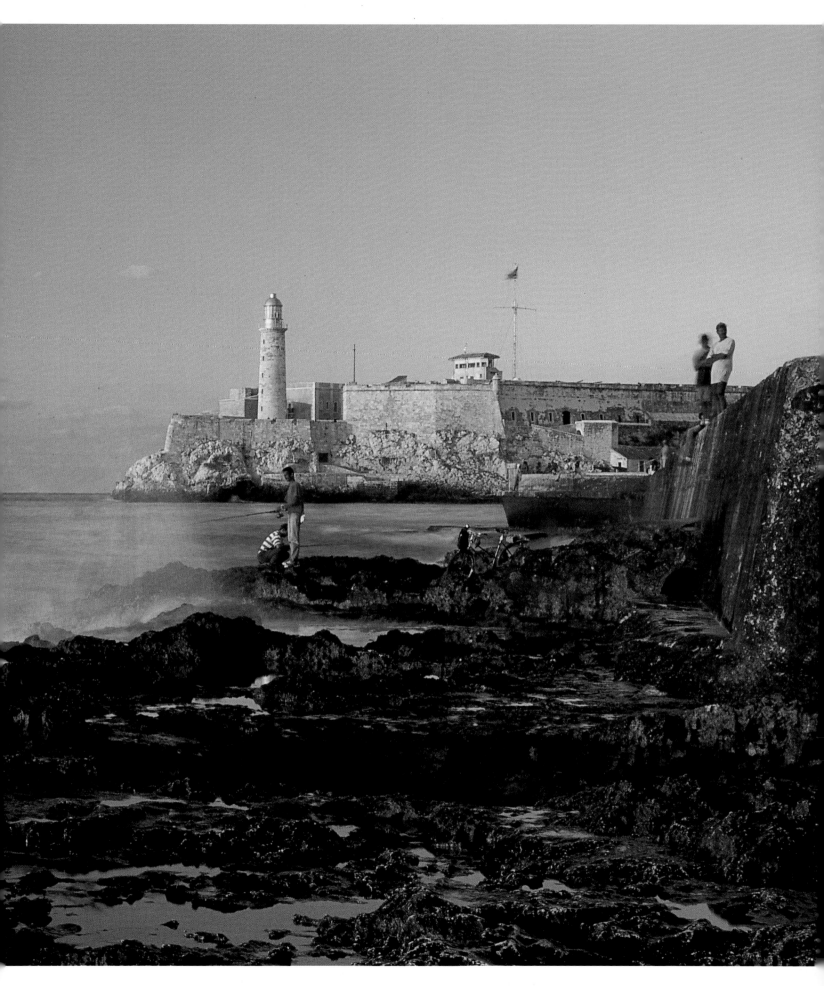

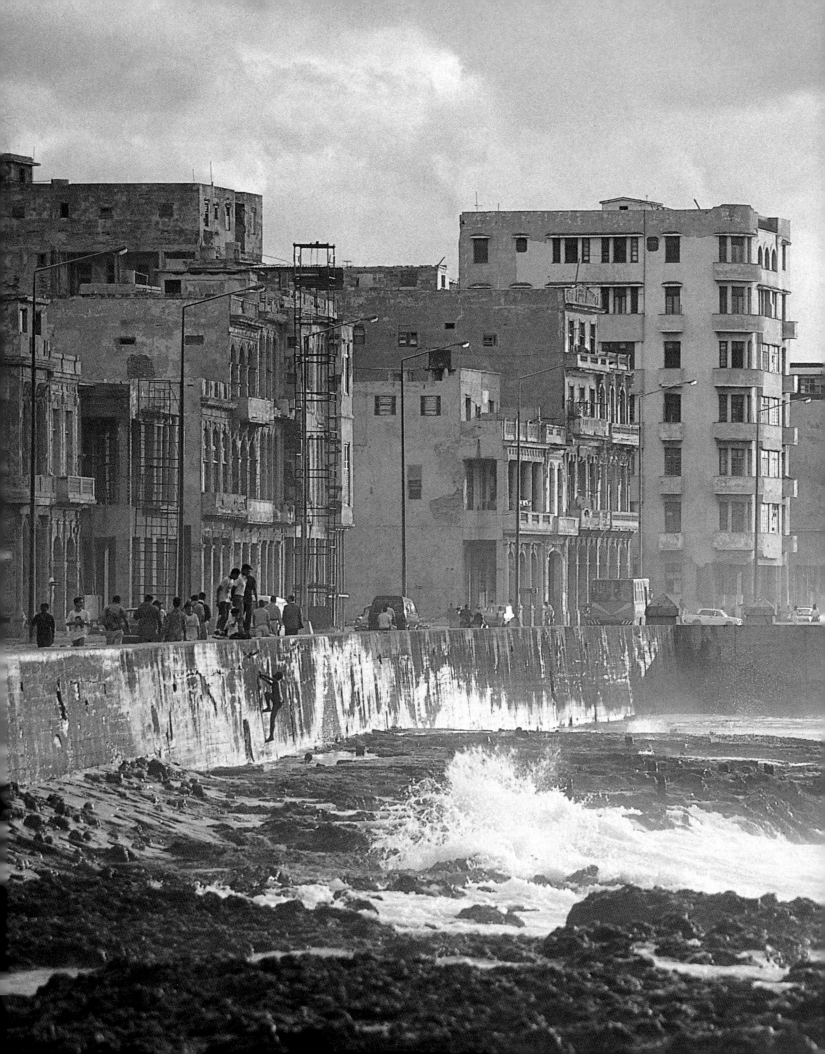

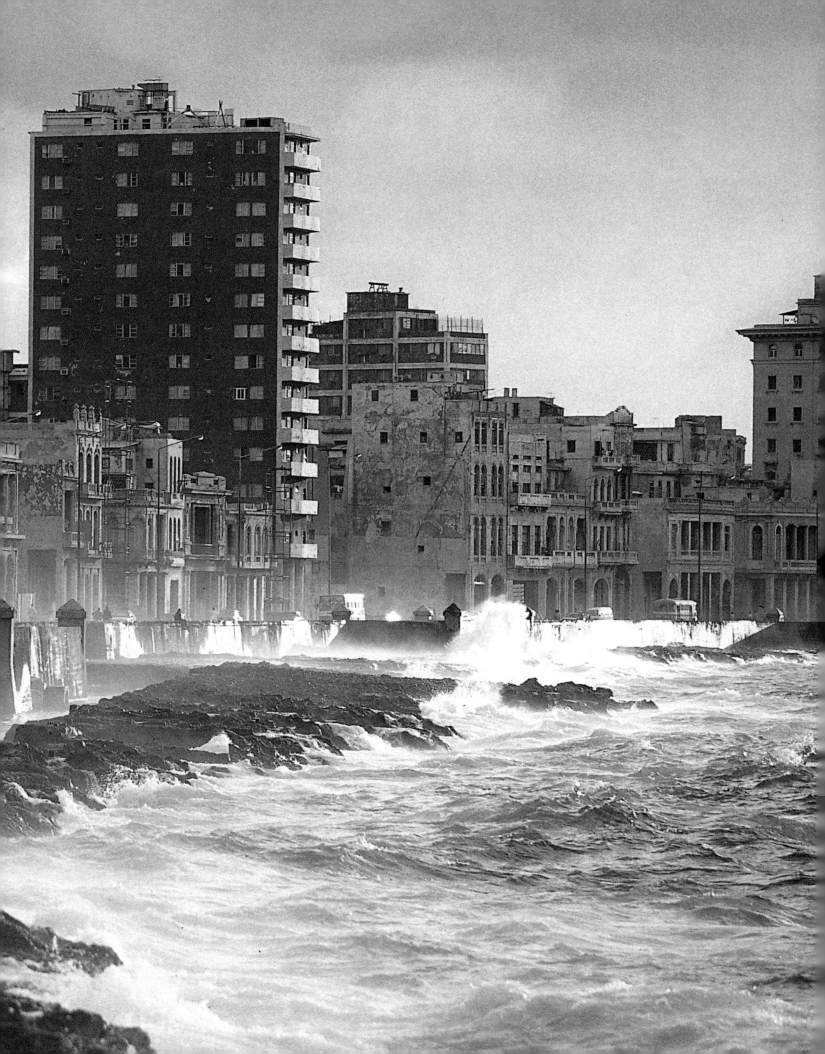

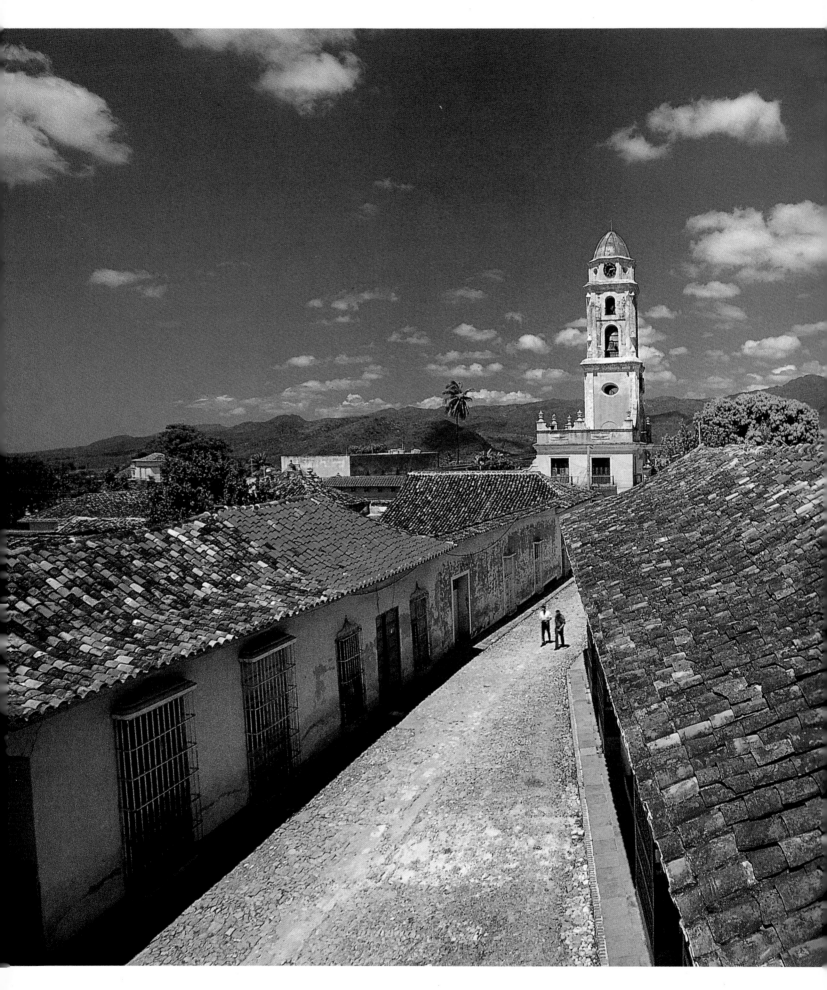

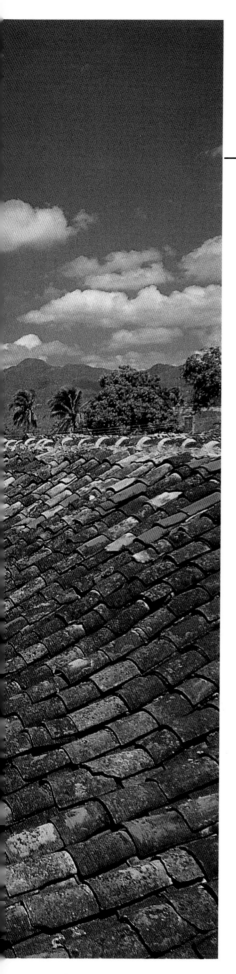

Trinidad, historic capital of sugar production

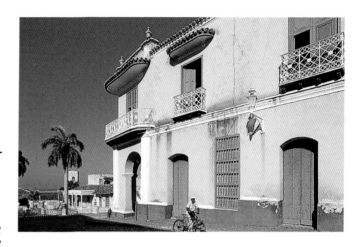

82-83 *Designated by UNESCO as a World Heritage Site, the town of Trinidad abounds in picturesque scenarios: delightful pastel-painted houses with red roofs and narrow cobbled streets leading to tiny squares dominated by beautiful little churches with tall bell-towers. And work on the restoration of Trinidad's unique colonial legacy continues.*

83 top *This building in Trinidad overlooks Plaza Mayor, visible in the background to the left. Its verdant courtyard is clad with tiles made in Bremen, Germany, and once used as a ship's ballast. Founded in 1514 by Diego Velázquez, Trinidad is the third oldest town on the island, after Baracoa and Bayamo. Its isolation over a period of almost two centuries did much to conserve its original layout and architecture.*

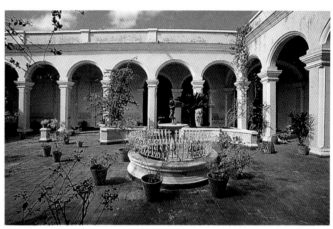

83 top center *This splendid patio belongs to the former residence of the Brunet family, wealthy sugarcane plantation owners who abandoned their business and the island after slavery was abolished. In 1974 the building became the Museo Romantico: its rooms, including an intriguing kitchen, are decorated with furnishings, pictures and other objects from several aristocratic homes. As a whole the museum offers a fascinating insight into everyday life in the colonial era.*

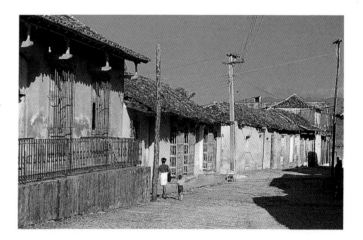

83 bottom center *Some of Trinidad's buildings are still in need of a facelift but work continues to restore the town's original appearance, with walls painted in warm pastel shades of yellow, pink, blue and green and windows protected by wooden* rejas *or wrought-iron grilles. Through them passers-by catch glimpses of paneled ceilings, walls finished with* azulejos *from Seville, the ubiquitous rocking chair and shady patios.*

83 bottom *Just 9 miles from Trinidad, this strange tower rises out of the fields of sugarcane. It is called the Torre de Iznaga, after a local family who once owned plantations here and who had it built – in this undeniably eclectic style – to oversee slaves and prevent them from fleeing. Nearby are a ruined farmhouse and remains of the old railway.*

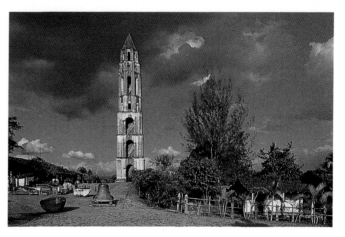

84 top *The rounded arches above the windows in this room in the Museo Romanico are known as* abanicos *(fans): they are an ingenious albeit simple system for ventilating rooms, letting light in or keeping it out.*

84 center left *Another room in the Museo Romantico. None of the furniture and objects that originally filled these rooms has survived; it was all scattered and lost after the building was abandoned. The present collection was put together by Carlos J. Zerquera, city historian, with acquisitions and donations from private individuals.*

84 center right *Another room in the Museo Romantico. Rocking chairs from Louisiana, mirrors from Venice, fragile French and German glasswares and bedspreads from Castille: all is now tastefully displayed in rooms with inlaid mahogany ceilings.*

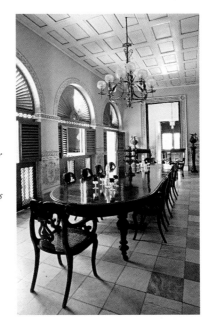

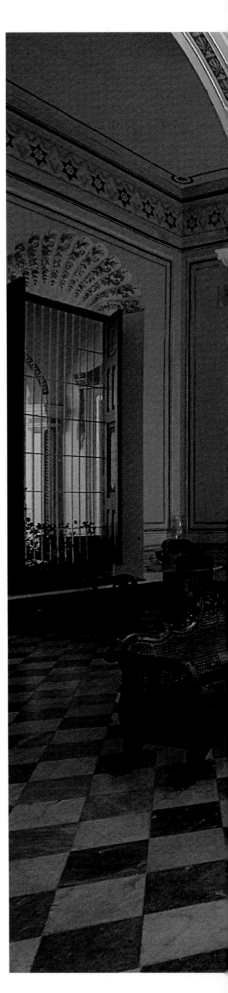

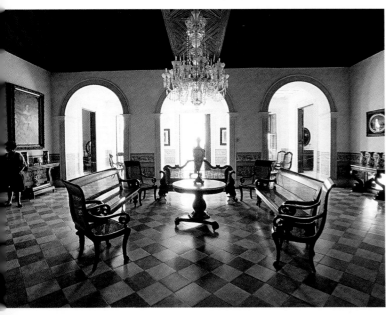

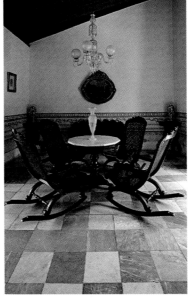

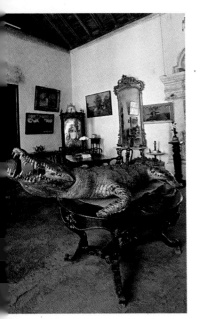

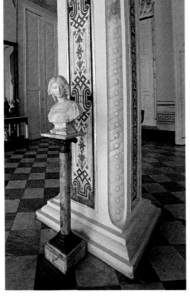

84 bottom left *This photo, taken in a private house in Trinidad, conveys a good idea of how homes were furnished, with a taste that verges on kitsch. Arranged in the traditional way beneath the panelled mahogany ceiling are assorted furniture and objects of European origin. But the most prominent place, at the center of the room, is occupied by a stuffed local crocodile.*

84 bottom right *Palacio Cantero in Trinidad, home of the Museo de Historia Municipal, offers a fine example of the exceptional restoration work done in the town. This photo shows the meticulous and delicate wall decorations.*

84-85 *Major episodes from Trinidad's history are preserved for posterity at the Museo de Historia Municipal, housed in the Palacio Cantero, built in 1810-1812 in Calle Bolivar.*

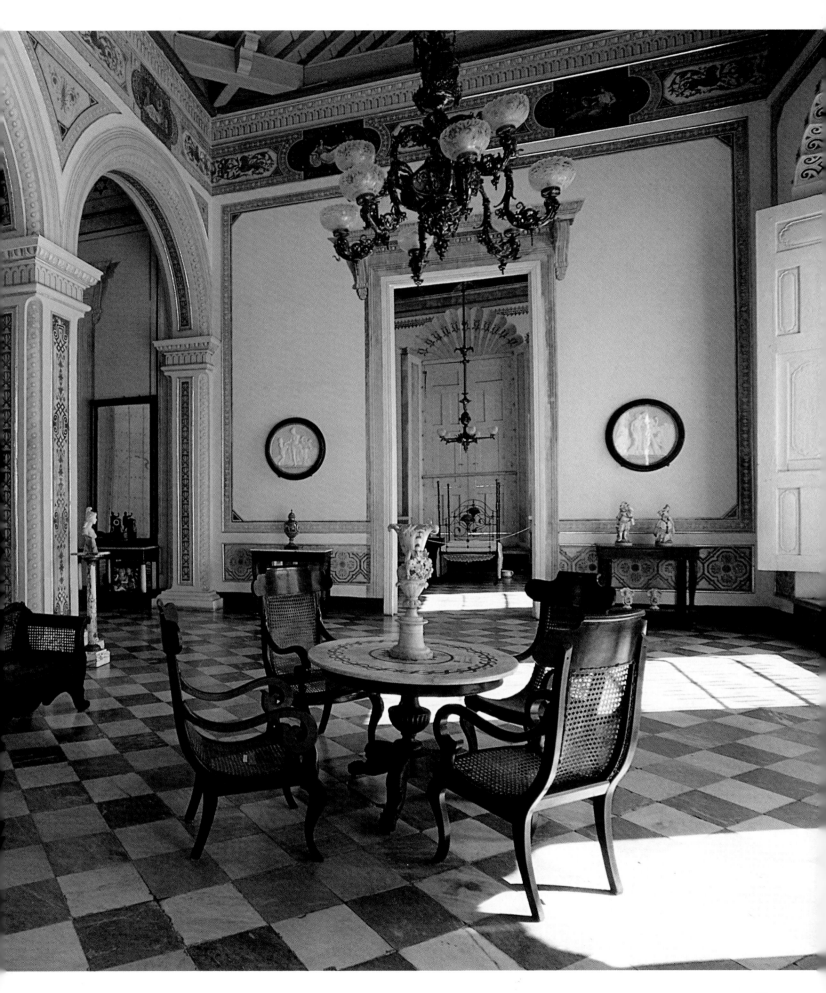

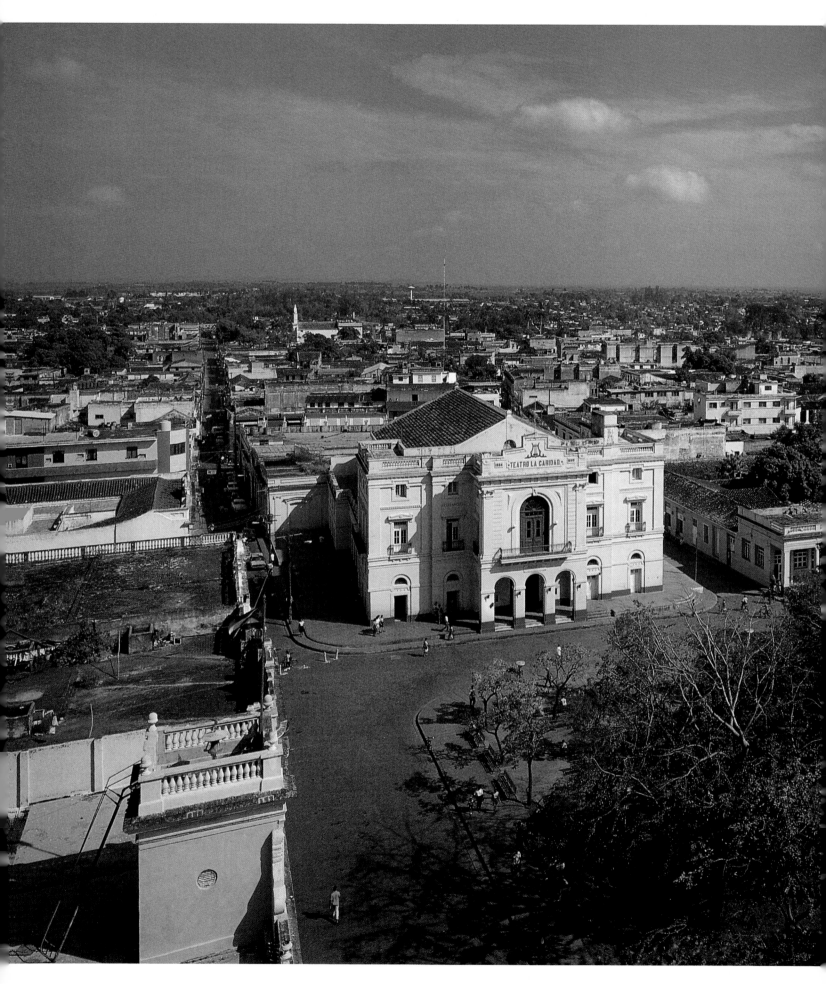

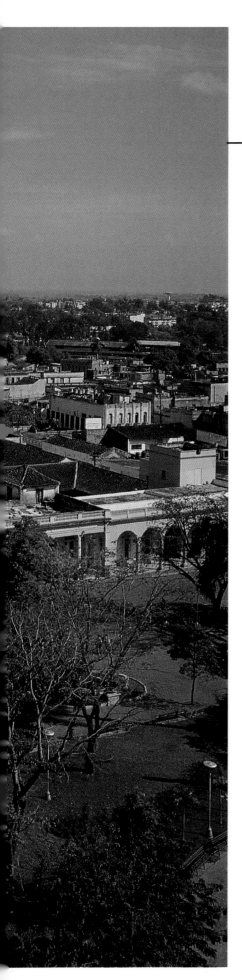

Santa Clara, agricultural heart of Cuba

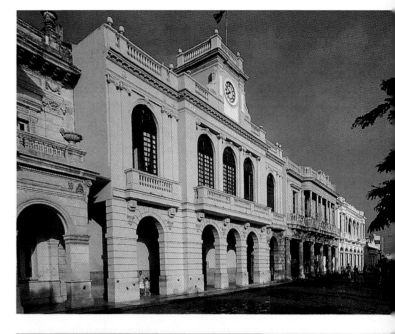

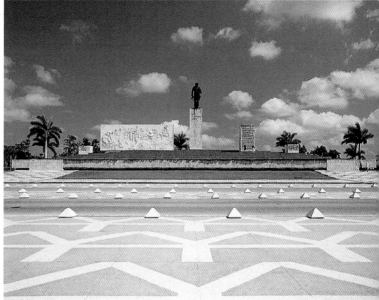

86-87 *Founded towards the end of the 17th century, Santa Clara – capital of Villa Clara province – enjoyed economic prosperity thanks to the area's sugarcane plantations. Today it is an industrial and university center. It also occupies a prominent place in the history of the Revolution: it was the scene, in 1958, of both fierce fighting between Batista's troops and guerillas led by Che Guevara and the celebrated attack on the government forces' Tren Blindado.*

87 top *Plaza Vidal in the town of Santa Clara is overlooked by handsome buildings dating to the late 19th/early 20th century. Among them are the Casa de la Trova, the Hotel Santa Clara Libre – its façade still marked by splinters of shells fired during the famous battle of 1958 – the Museum of Decorative Arts and the Caridad Theater, founded by the wealthy Abreu family for less fortunate townspeople. In 1878 the same family set up Santa Clara's first free clinic and an elementary school.*

87 bottom *Dominating Plaza de la Revolución, south of central Santa Clara, is a large bronze statue of Che Guevara in combat gear, over the words "Hasta la Victoria Siempre". Displayed in the nearby museum are maps, uniforms, documents, weapons and the first rudimentary transmission equipment employed by Radio Rebelde, which was installed in Che Guevara's mountain base at La Mesa, in the Sierre del Escambray.*

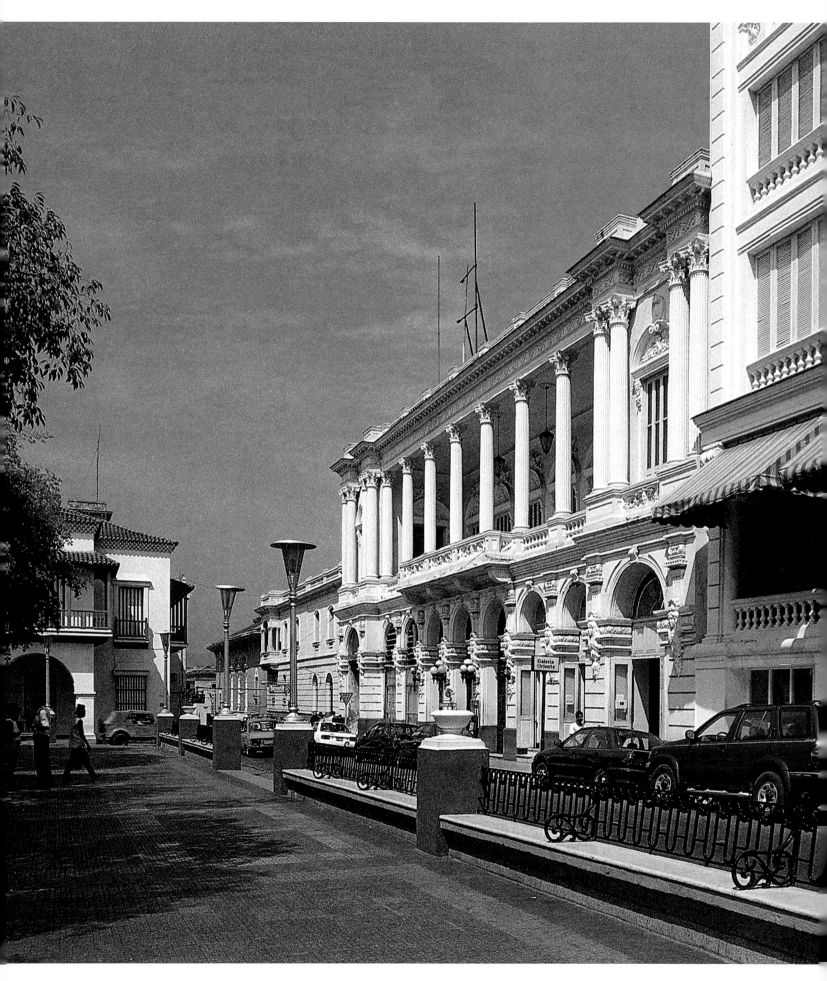

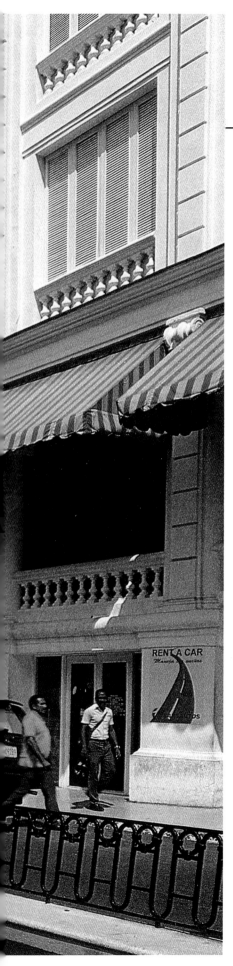

Santiago, cradle of the revolution

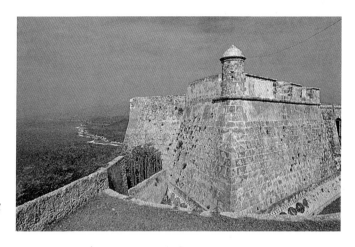

88-89 *Santiago de Cuba is considered the most Caribbean and exotic of the island's cities, populated by a mixture of races. In the 18th century many Haitians, both black and white, fled from their own island and took refuge here. It is Cuba's second city in terms of size and is known for its colonial architecture, as this picture shows. Founded by the Spanish in 1514, it was the island's capital until 1549.*

89 top *Perched on steep cliffs fringing the bay south of the city is the Castillo del Morro, designed by the Italian architect Antonelli and built in 1710. At different times in its history this imposing and gloomy structure was used as a temporary accommodation for slaves bound for the plantations and as a prison. It is reached across a drawbridge. The fortress now contains an interesting museum of piracy through the ages.*

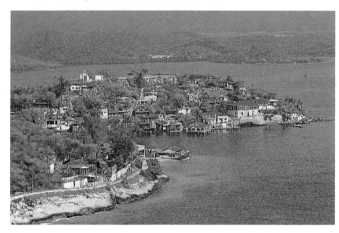

89 top center *The Castillo del Morro offers a fine vantage point for views over the Caribbean, the distant spurs of the Sierra Maestra and the island of Cayo Granma. This tiny island was once called Smith, after the rich British slave trader who owned it. It is now named after the boat used by Castro and his followers when they landed in Cuba in 1956.*

89 bottom center *Casa de Velázquez, built between 1516 and 1530 on Parque Céspedes, was in effect once occupied by the governor who used the ground floor as a trading office and the first floor as his private residence. After a period as a hotel, it eventually became the Museo de Arte Colonial, with collections of tapestries, paintings, furniture and ceramics brought to Cuba by the Spanish. Opening onto its patio – amid blue-painted walls – are casement doors with white shutters, surmounted by fanlights (abanicos) decorated with multi-colored stained glass.*

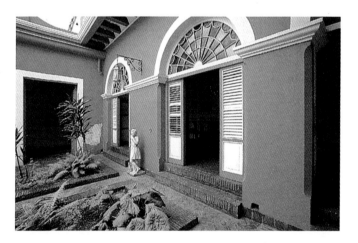

89 bottom *This red American automobile from the '50s is one of thousands – Buicks, Packards, Chevrolets, Chryslers, Studebakers, Hudsons, Edsels, Fords – that are still running on Cuba's roads, like colorful ghosts of U.S. capitalism, built at a time when cars were still made to last. Fidel Castro himself used to drive around the island in a luxurious Oldsmobile, while Che Guevara's Chevy figures large in Havana's vintage car museum.*

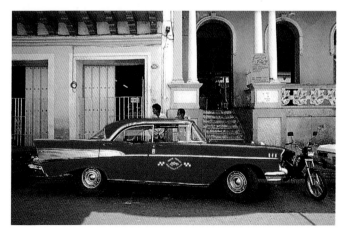

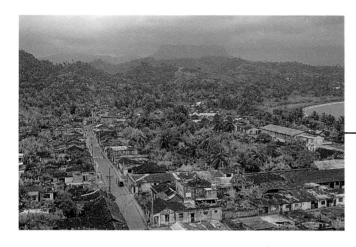

Coymar and its sisters

90 top *Baracoa, founded by Diego Velázquez in 1512, is Cuba's oldest town. Christopher Columbus landed in the area on October 27th 1492 and spent a week there. Thanks to its position, off the main trade routes, Baracoa's baroque and colonial features have remained intact, with a cathedral dating from the year of its foundation. The town is dominated by El Yunque mountain, covered by dense forests. Important pre-Columbian archaeological finds have been made nearby.*

90 top center *Camaguey is at the center of a rich sugar-producing and cattle-farming area. It boasts some interesting baroque monuments, among them the cathedral, the Iglesia de Nuestra Senora de la Soledad and the building now occupied by the law courts. Along the streets a particular note of local color is provided by the* tinajones: *gigantic earthenware containers once used to collect rainwater. The town also has two museums: one on the Revolution, in the Casa de Ignacio Agramonte, the other in the Casa de Jesus Suarez Gayol.*

90 bottom center *The fishing village of Cojimar, about 7 miles from Havana, provided Ernest Hemingway with material for his novel* The Old Man and the Sea. *As a sign of gratitude, the local people had a neoclassical monument built and dedicated to the writer; it contains a bust made from the metal of boat engines donated by the local fishermen. The monument stands opposite a Spanish fort, now used to garrison troops.*

90 bottom *A huge poster lauds the Revolution at the entrance to the village of Playa Giron, on the Bahìa de Cochinos, the famous Bay of Pigs where 1,500 counter-revolutionaries, trained by the CIA, made an unsuccessful invasion attempt in 1961. This major episode in Cuba's recent history is commemorated by 80 inscribed stones along the road between the two places and a small museum with a collection of documents, photos, arms and other items.*

90-91 *The site of present-day Cienfuegos was long ignored. It was settled only in the 19th century, when an aristocratic Frenchman who had lived in New Orleans persuaded some inhabitants of Bordeaux to move there. Cienfuegos, now a thriving industrial city, is named after a general (its original name was Fernandina de Jagua).*

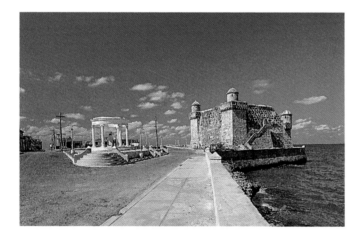

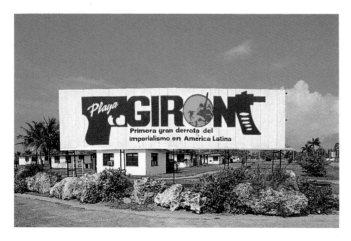

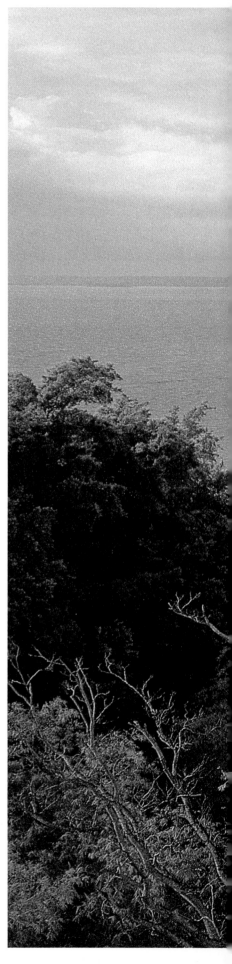

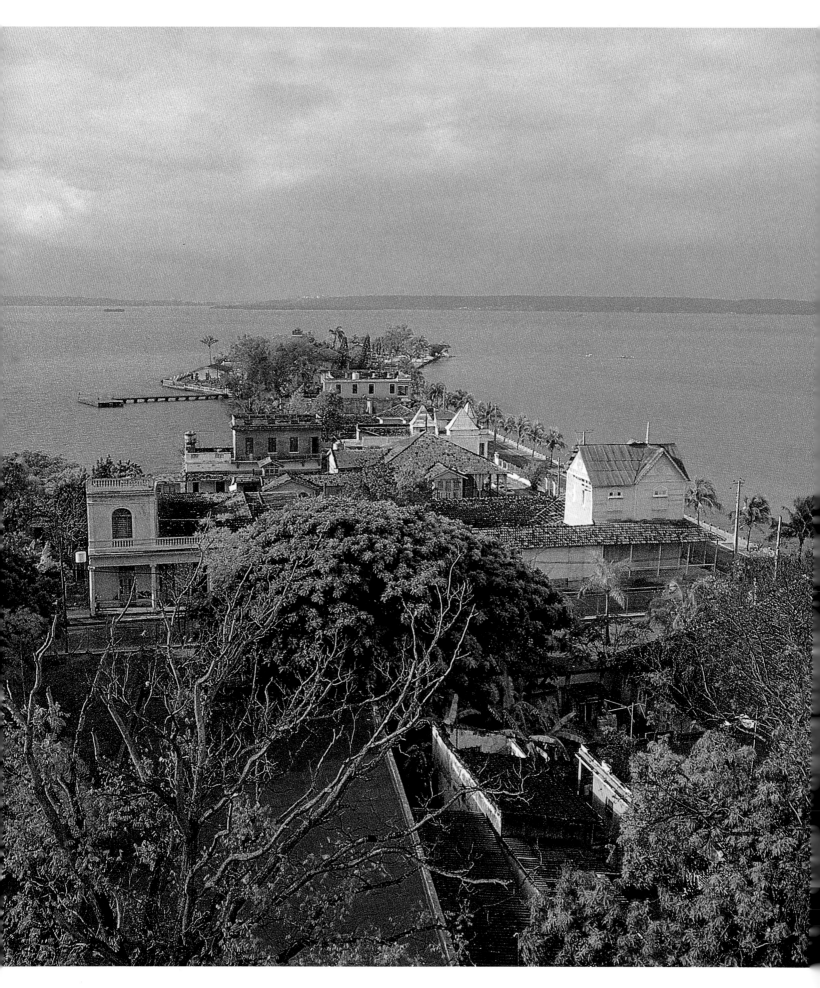

Varadero, alias Miami

92 top left *The pools of Varadero's hotels – like this one at the Hotel Meliá – have the kind of features more often associated with Hollywood: heated water, for slightly cooler spring and autumn days; miniature waterfalls and even waves; bars you swim to, right in the center, for a delicious rum cocktail – a mojito or daiquiri, perhaps – to sip and savor while relaxing in the pool.*

92 right *Hotels in other tourist areas of Cuba besides Varadero – where the Hotel Meliá, depicted in this photo, is located – often have a common architectural feature: a tall central tower with a patio overlooked by corridors or rooms. The surrounding walls are entirely covered by hanging greenery, and the charm of the ambience is enhanced by the gentle sound of cascading water. Completing this verdant scene are the trees and plants that decorate the lobby.*

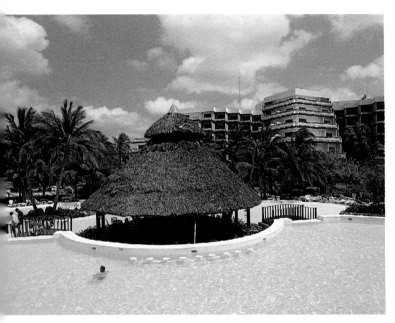

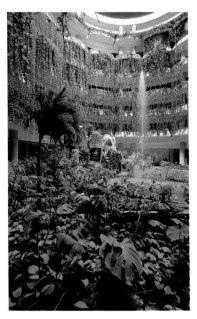

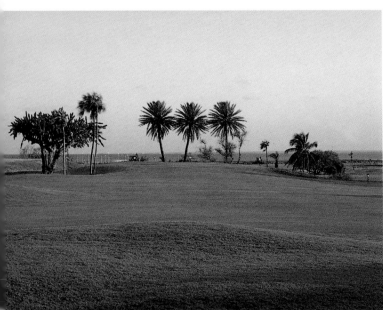

92 bottom left *The golf course at Varadero dates from the period before the Revolution, when developers already saw the benefits of providing vacation resorts with sports facilities. Varadero now offers all the leisure activities holiday-makers look for: water sports, horse-riding and bicycles with which to reach more isolated beaches, away from the crowds that pack the waterfront by the hotels.*

92-93 *Seen from a distance, the Meliá Hotel looks vaguely like an Aztec pyramid. Launched by the American millionnaire Dupont back in the 1930s, the now-famous tourist resort of Varadero, in Matanzas province, is a popular package tour destination, offering amenities of every kind: mega-hotels and luxury villas, stunning beaches and huge pools, restaurants and sports facilities and night-life in abundance.*

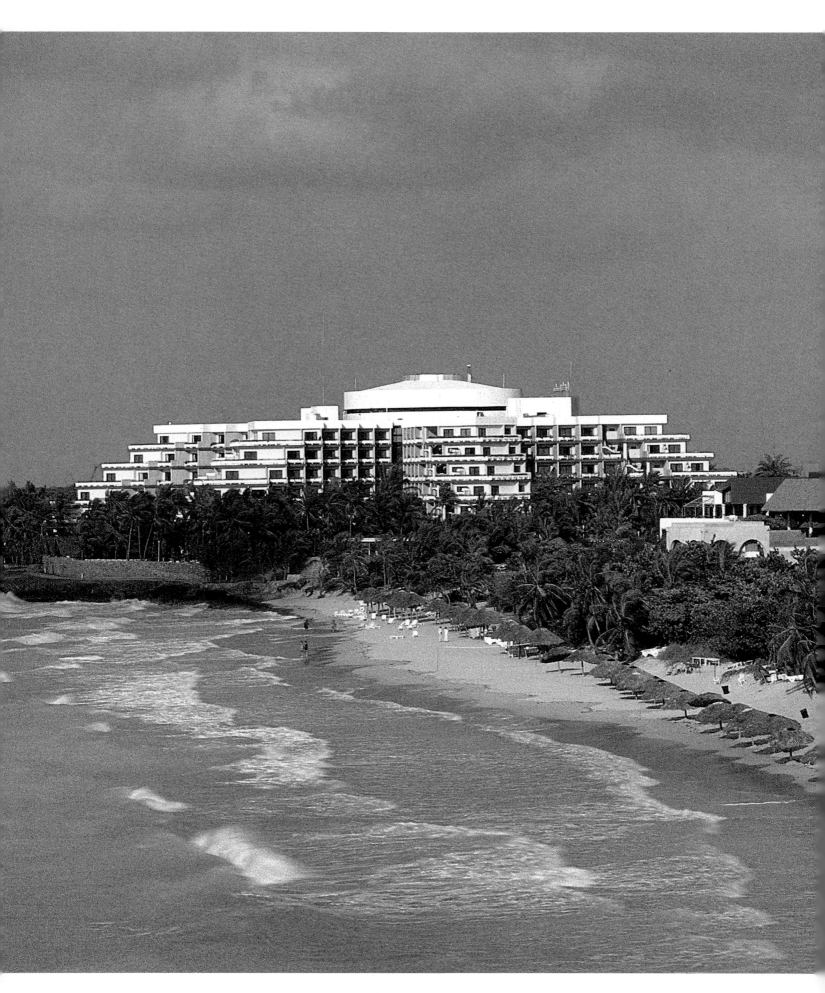

A celebration of multiethnicity

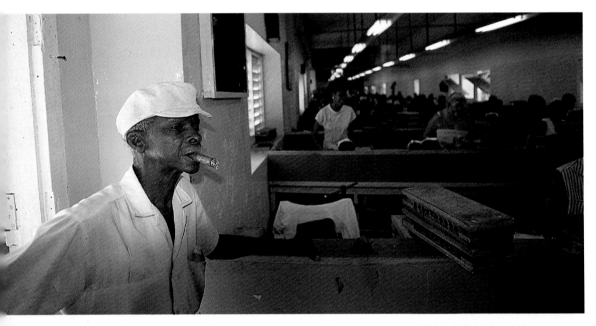

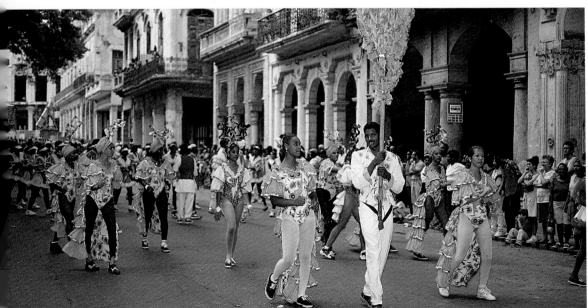

94 top *Making cigars is a job done in factories by skilled workers. The wrapper leaf is removed from the damp cloth it has been kept in, then spread on a table; after its edges have been cut, it is carefully rolled, measured with a ruler and then placed with the bundled filler. This is the "tube"; the top and bottom are then made and stuck to the tube with special gum.*

94 bottom *On the island of Cuba, Carnival is staged several times during the year. The traditional occasion is the sugarcane harvest in summer, generally in July. But for the sake of tourism, festivities have also been brought into line with the international carnival calendar, with celebrations held in January or February. This applies particularly in places where tourism plays a major role.*

95 *In the impervious regions of the Sierra del Escambray, horses are still the best way to get around. They are also a great help to farmers. This photo of horse and rider was taken near the village of Manicaragua, where the road forks in the directions of Trinidad, Sancti Spiritus and the reservoir of Hanabanilla. The huge lake formed by the waters of the Hanabanilla river is now a popular tourist attraction.*

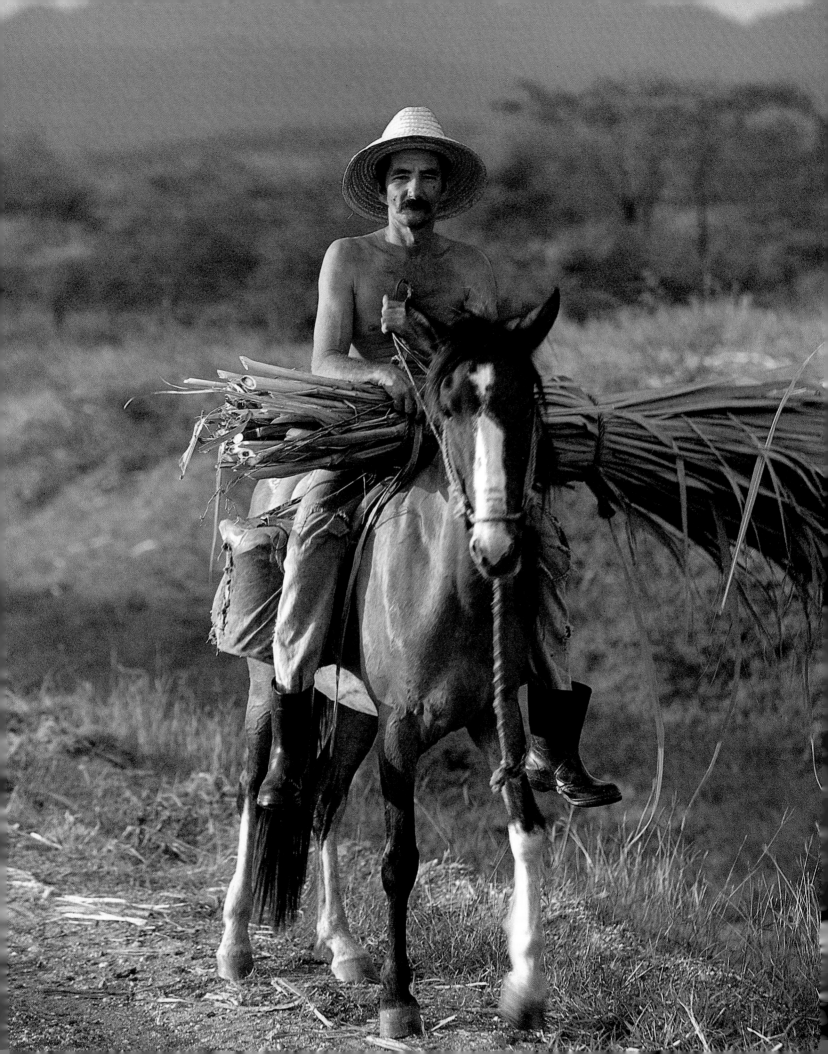

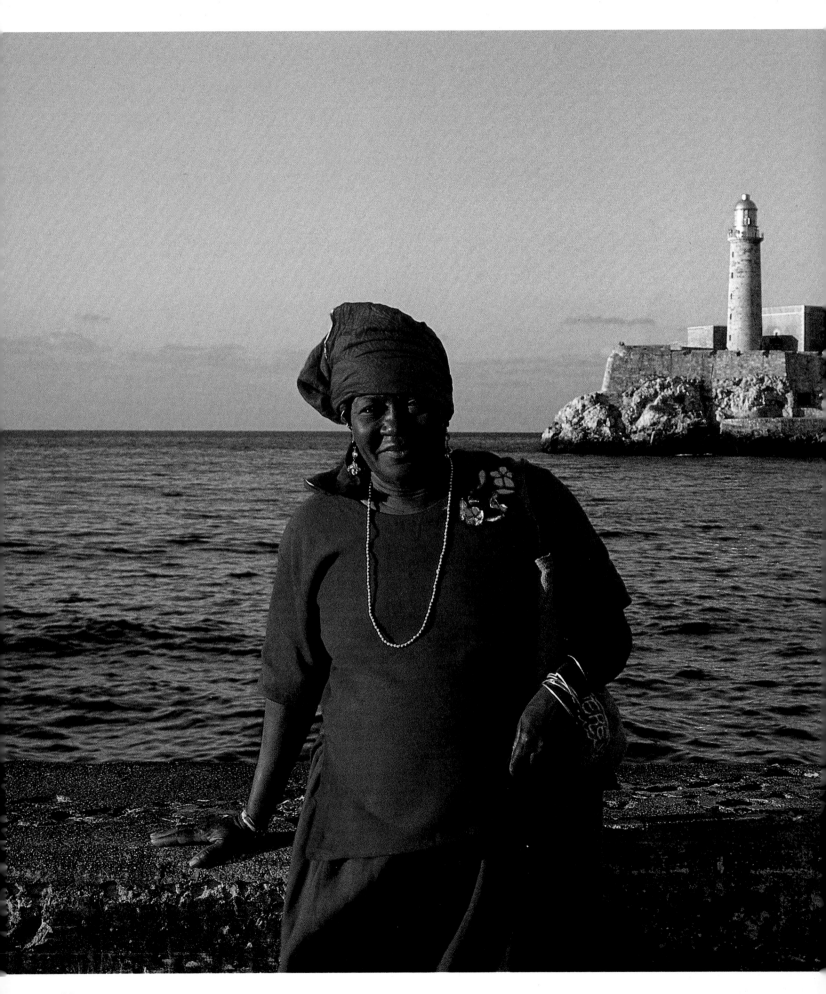

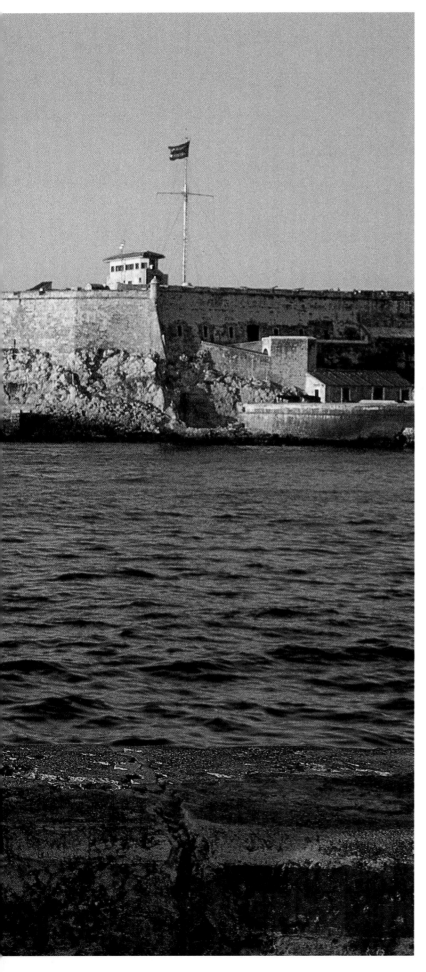

96-97 *Leaning against a wall, with the Castillo del Morro behind her, a Cuban woman smiles at the camera in the light of the setting sun. Her outfit – complete with turban, necklace, bracelet and earrings – could be everyday wear or "Sunday best". The Cubans show a lot of respect for women like her, who may have raised as many as six or eight children, with a spirit of sacrifice and a strong sense of dignity.*

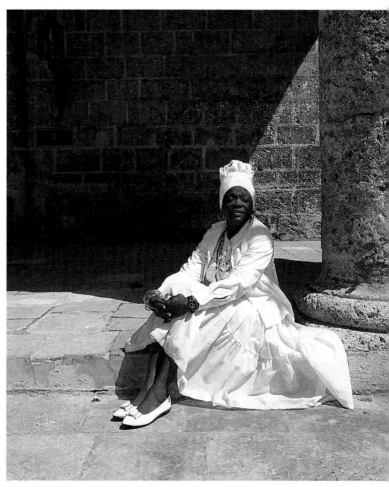

97 *The Santería cult is one of the mysteries and great passions of Cuba. Consisting essentially of the syncretism of Roman Catholicism and traditional African beliefs, it was adopted out of necessity to avoid persecution and accusations of heresy directed against individuals who publicly worshipped the* orichas, *African deities. The photo shows a priestess wearing the typical white clothes.*

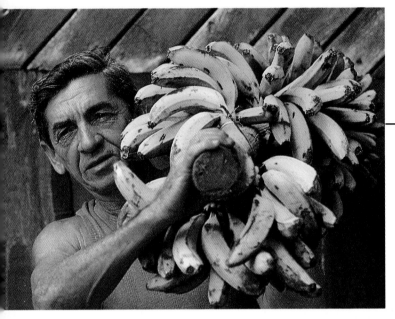

A day in "sugarland"

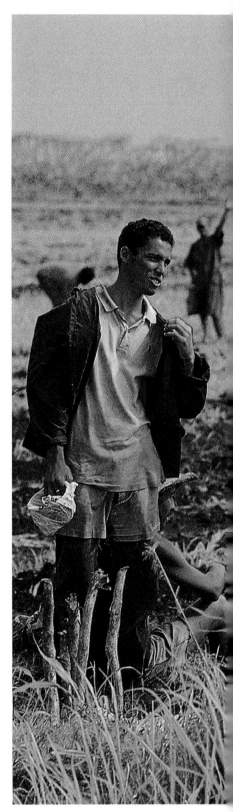

98 top left *In a country best known for tobacco and sugarcane it comes as a surprise to see pictures like this one. Banana groves may not be very common but the bananas they produce are exceptionally good.*

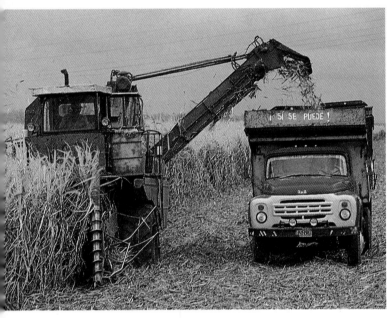

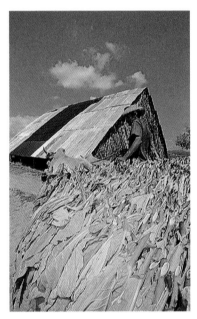

98 center left *Sugarcane was once cut entirely by hand with machetes, heavy knives with curved blades. Nowadays, even in Cuba where mechanization is still limited, part of the work is done by machines that cut, collect and stack the canes in large trucks as this photo, taken in Holguín, shows.*

98 bottom left *When the tobacco leaves are ready for picking, it's time for the vaqueros of Pinar del Río province to get to work. It looks like a simple task but tobacco-growing is labor-intensive and the plants demand as much attention as grape vines. Sowing starts in November and continues until the end of February; leaves are picked every five or seven days, over a period of three to four months. When picking is over, the ground must be left fallow.*

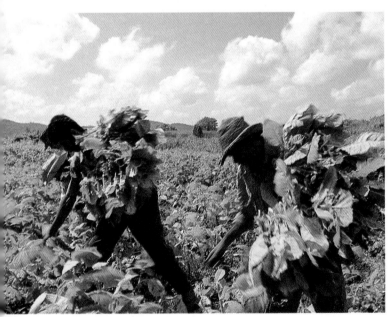

98 right *A farmers' hut in Villa Clara province is used to store the harvest. Its structure resembles the dwellings of the pre-Columbian Indians, exterminated by the conquistadores. There was an indigenous population of at least 100,000: Siboneyes and Guanahuatabeyes, nomadic tribes that survived from hunting and fishing, and Tainos, sedentary tribes of farmers.*

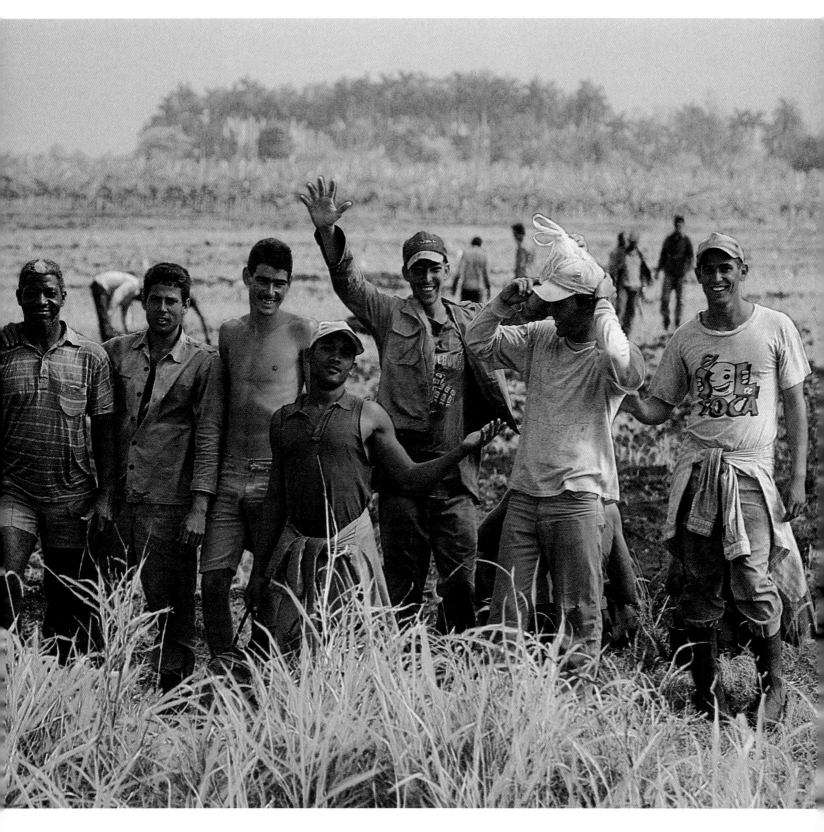

98-99 *Matanzas province is considered by many to represent the real Cuba, thanks also to its many facets: tourism (Varadero), oil refining (Càrdenas), sugar production (Puerto Rico Libre), scenic landscapes (Parque Natural de la Ciénaga de Zapata and Cueva de Bellamar), and history (sites of battles fought in the war for independence). Agriculture is a mainstay of the local economy and people travelling through the countryside are often greeted with a wave from peasants working in the fields.*

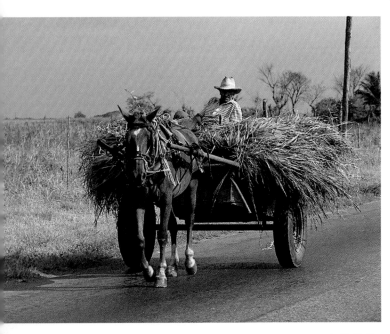

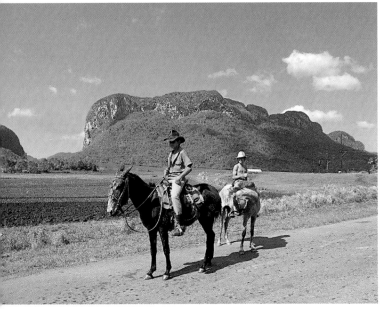

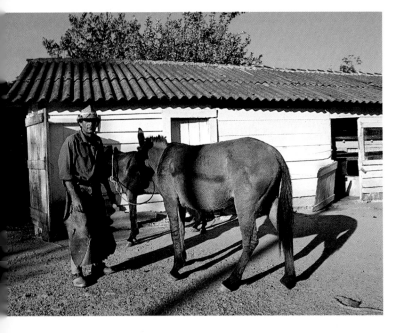

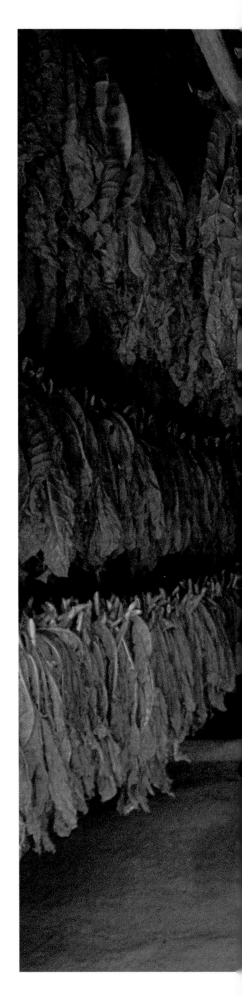

100 top *Matanzas province owes its prosperity to three crops: sugarcane, tobacco and coffee. Here farming techniques have changed little through the centuries, with machinery still far from replacing manual labor. For transport too, widespread use is still made of carts drawn by horses or other animals. The pace of work is slow, as it used to be in the rural communities of the Western world.*

100 center *Still today, in the countryside of Viñales, land is measured not in acres but in caballerìas: a unit of measurement based on the distance a horse can cover in a set time. And horses are still the means of transport used by the majority of tobacco farmers to get around their huge plantations.*

100 bottom *Men often have a very special relationship with the animal that does most to help them work and carry things from place to place. Particularly in out-of-the-way regions of the Sierra del Escambray – where there are no highways but only paths and dirt roads – a horse is a precious and irreplaceable companion, tireless and uncomplaining.*

100-101 *As soon as they are picked, the still moist tobacco leaves are hung on poles arranged crosswise in the drying houses and cured there for several months. These wooden structures with thatched roofs have no windows, so the leaves remain in complete darkness. In Cuba cigars are a highly appreciated gift, especially when offered at the end of a meal. They are known by their brand name; the term "Havana" is used only outside Cuba.*

102-103 *Unlike Varadero, tourist resort par excellence, the interior of the Matanzas region is still frontier country, where* vaqueros *move around on horseback, decked out in their finest gear. Pastureland and a good climate make this an ideal place for cattle farms. In the second half of the 19th century Matanzas province was already among the most fertile in Cuba, accounting for, among other things, half the island's sugar production.*

104-105 *The ranches of Sancti Spiritus province are in some ways reminiscent of the Far West: although Cuba's main crops are sugarcane and tobacco, cattle farming is also important for the island's economy. Horses are reared to be saddled and ridden. And the essentially rural nature of this province is evident even in the capital, where it is not unusual to see* campesinos *on horseback.*

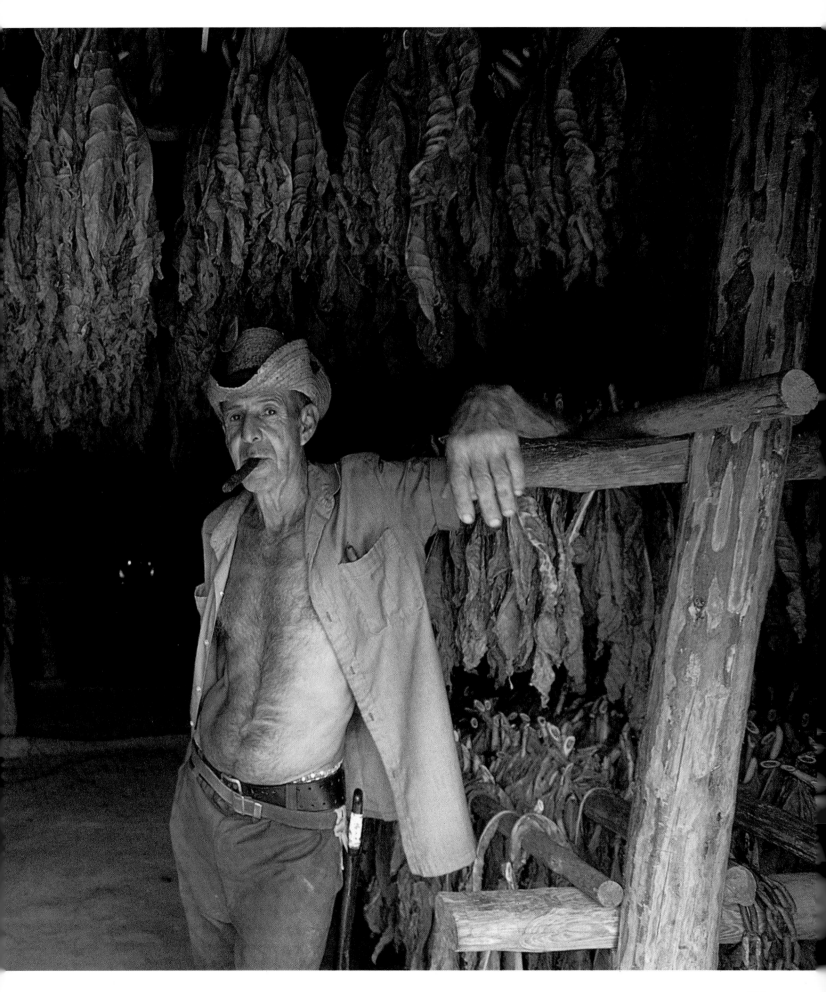

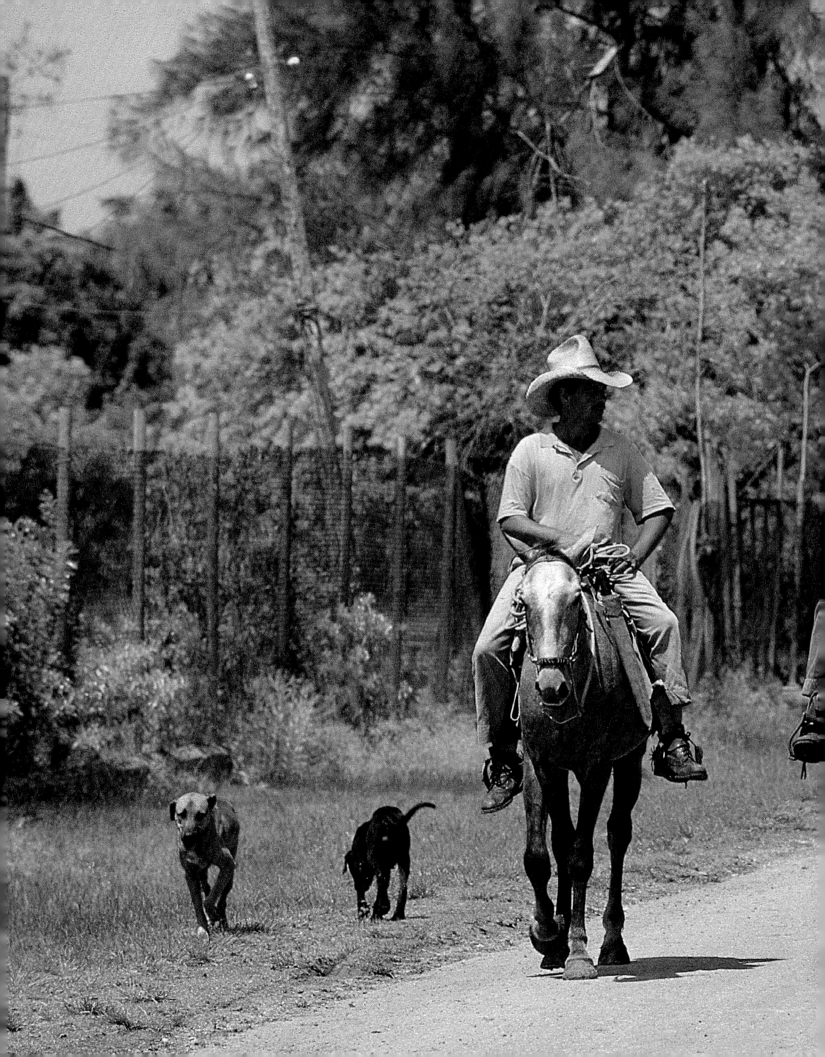

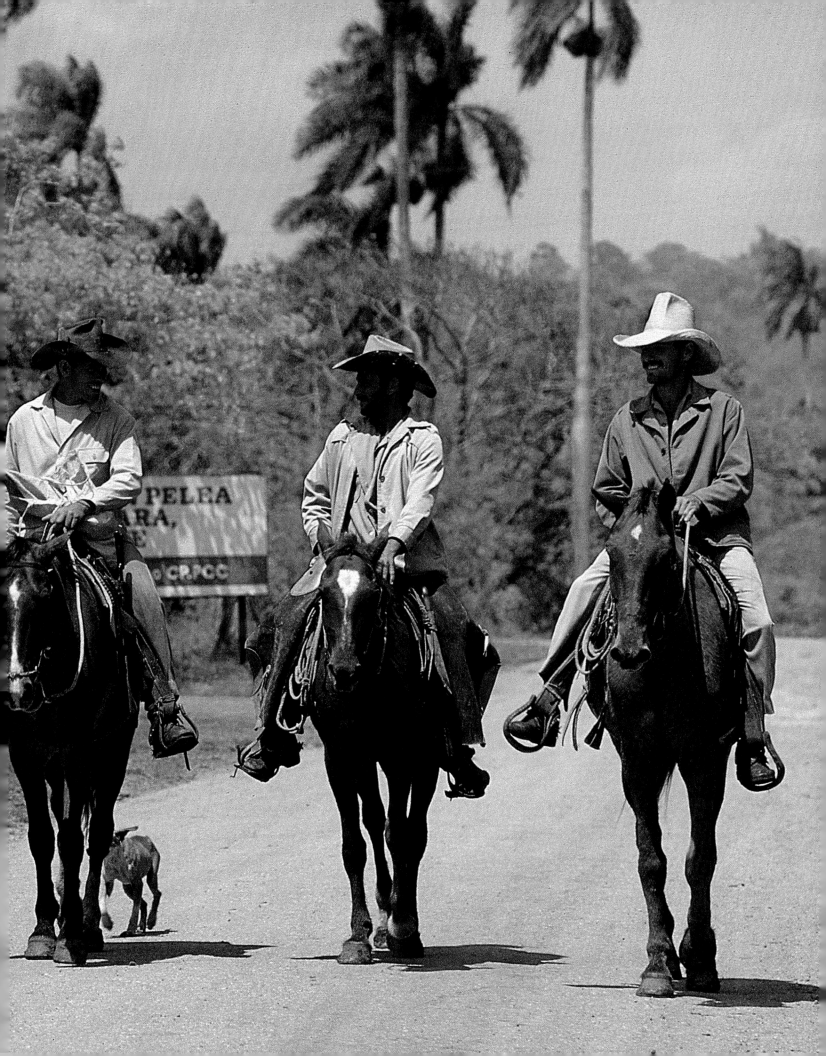

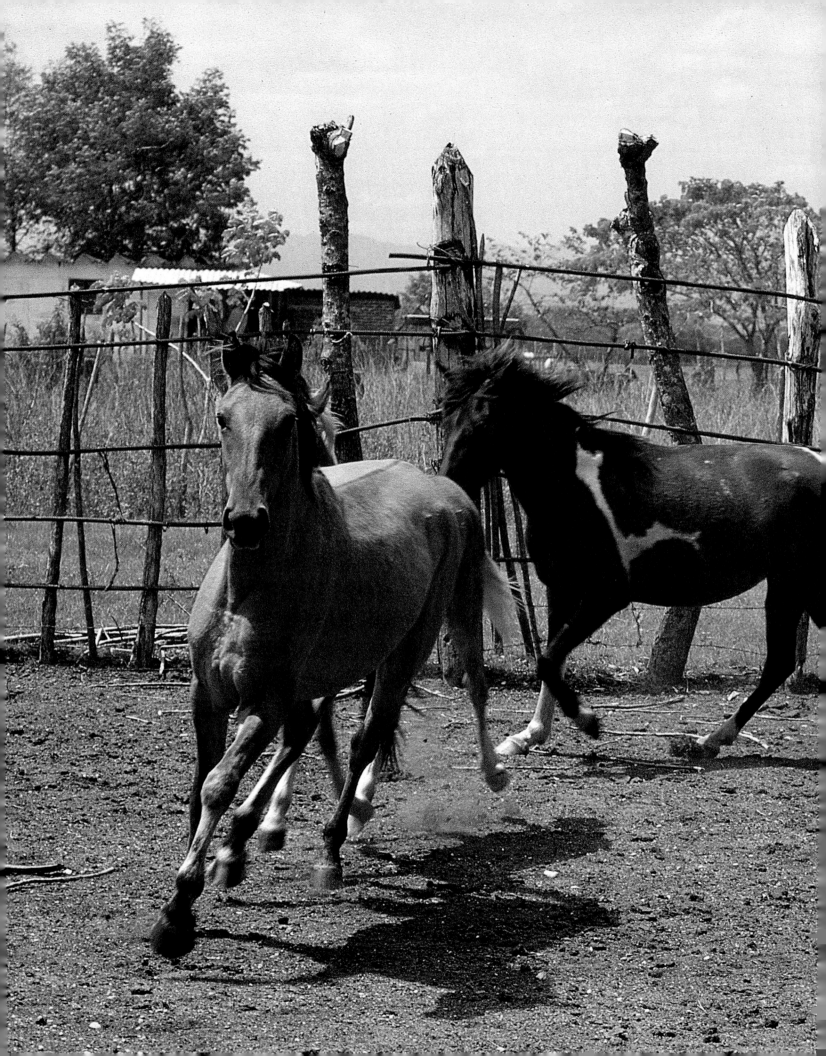

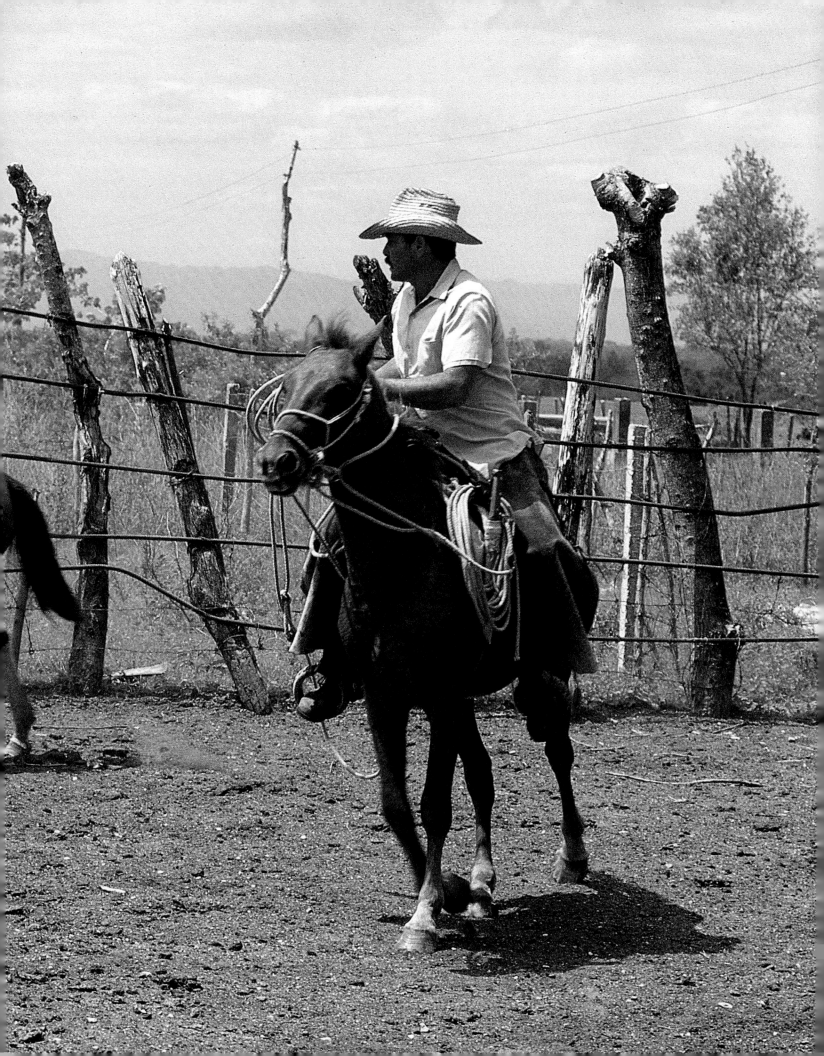

Cigars, flowers and Antillean beauties

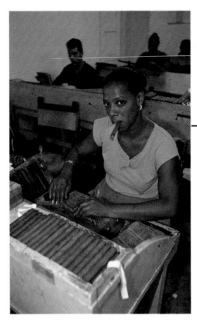

106 top *A* tabacalera *at her table, in the Viñales region. A characteristic figure in cigar factories is the so-called lector, a worker assigned the task of reading stories and poetry aloud during the working day, undeniably a great union victory of the last century. Nowadays the* lectores *have, for the most part, been replaced by the radio. But in many factories the newspaper is still read aloud by one of the workers every morning.*

106 bottom *It could be the tropical air, so mild and fragrant, or their natural disposition but the girls of Havana – and throughout the island of Cuba – are exceptionally cheerful and friendly. From a very early age they get accustomed to being in school groups and taking part in public events, ready to lead an independent life when the time comes.*

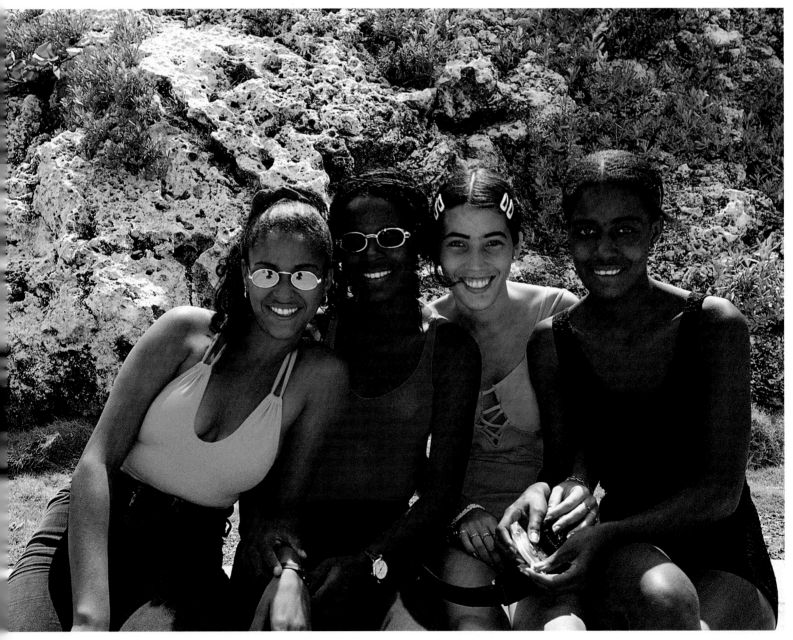

107 top The great majority of Cuba's ten million people are mestizos: less than a third of the population are "white" while the remainder are a typically Caribbean mix of Afro-European ethnic groups. The island's culture is also strongly influenced by the "black continent". As in much of the Antilles, and Brazil too, semi-religious rites of African origin have been preserved: combined with Catholicism they have produced forms of syncretism like Santería, the faith practised by the women seen in this photo.

107 bottom This man from Ciego de Avila province travels around on his bike selling sunflowers. Such a sight would have been unthinkable only a few years ago when the regime allowed no forms of private enterprise. Now times have changed and the Cubans vie with one another to devise new ways to make ends meet.

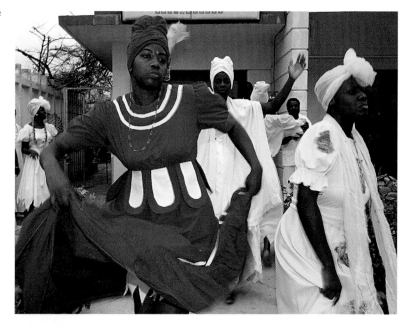

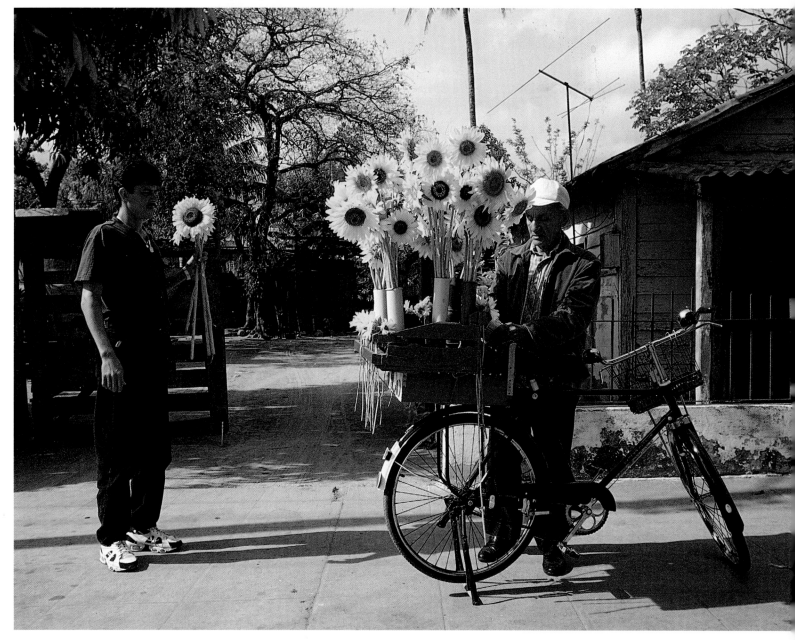

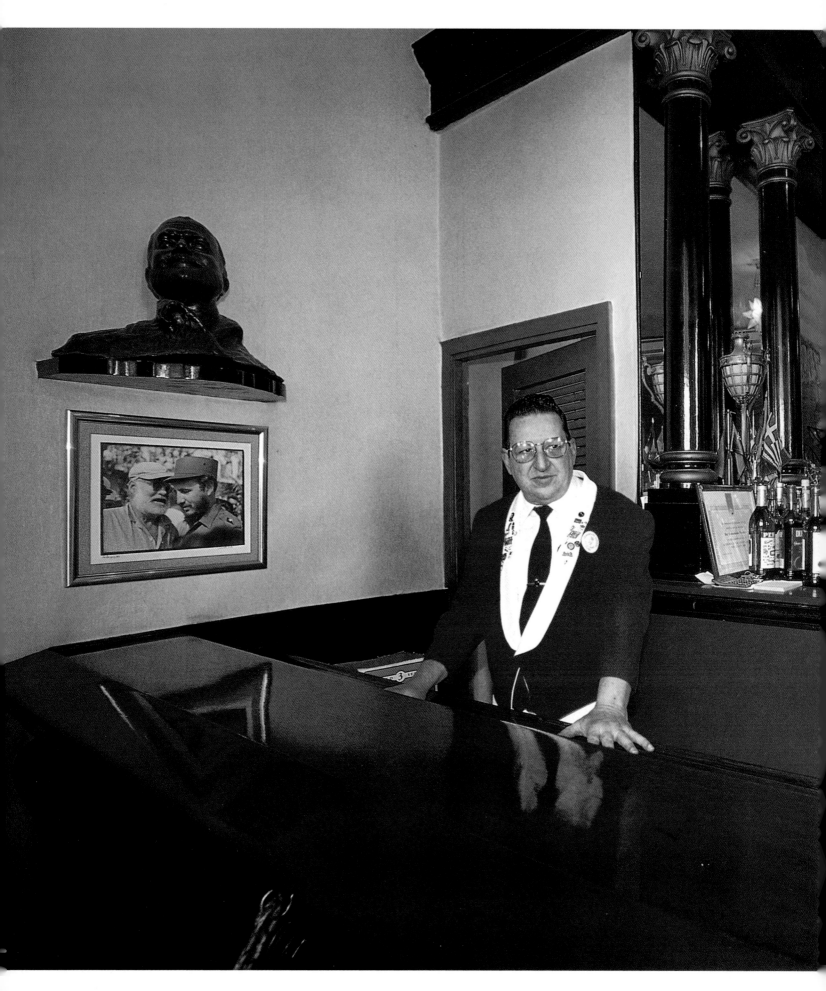

Caribbean traditions, American taste

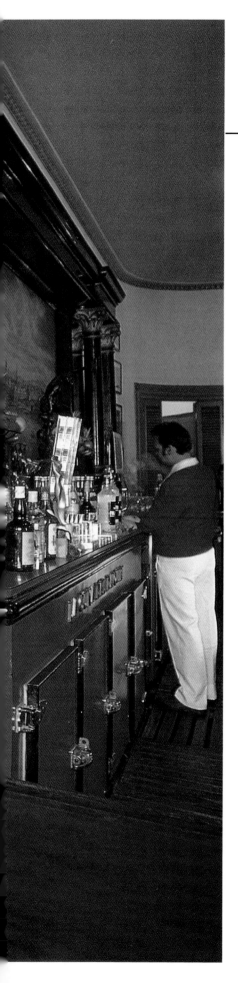

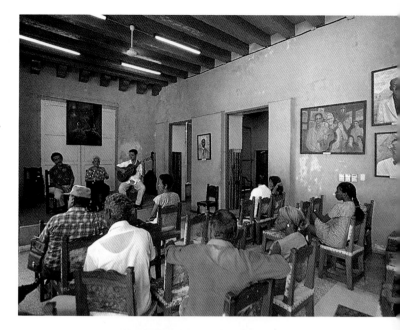

108-109 *Havana's celebrated El Floridita is a luxury restaurant and bar, best known as one of Ernest Hemingway's favorite haunts (there is a bust of the writer by the place where he used to sit). In 1953 Esquire magazine described the restaurant as one of the world's finest. Perhaps it was a bit different then. But even if its former charm disappeared with the recent restructuring, the quality of the food served there – and, above all, of the daiquiris mixed there – is still very high.*

109 top *The Casa de la Trova has existed in Santiago de Cuba since the 18th century. Music lovers gather here to listen to groups and soloists who perform in the daytime and evenings; guitarists, percussionists, both professional and amateur, perform. Saloon-style wooden doors, posters and photos on the walls and the generally warm, Bohemien ambience make this one of the most pleasant places in town to while away an evening.*

109 center *Bands like this one, formed mainly of string and percussion instruments (often of a fairly rudimentary kind), are common in Trinidad, as in every single town across the island, for the Cubans are passionately fond of all types of music. In Trinidad bands play in the Casa de la Trova, where the music tends to be more cultured, and at the Canchànchara, a tourist bar where there's live entertainment.*

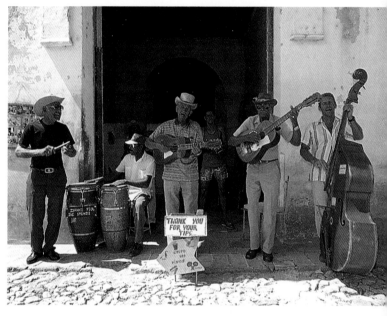

109 bottom *In Santiago de Cuba – as in Havana and elsewhere in the island – the roads are still dotted with cars manufactured in the USA back in the '50s, resplendent with their amazing aerodynamic bodywork, streamlined styling, running boards and bold colors. What we now see as an attractive feature of urban landscapes stemmed not from choice but from necessity, in the difficult years that followed the Revolution.*

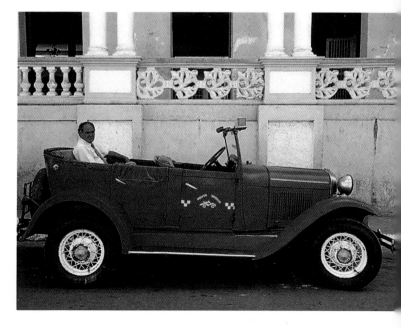

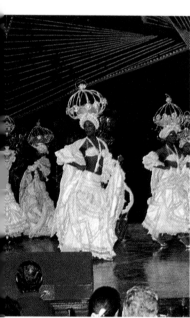

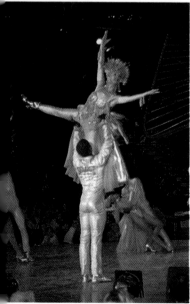

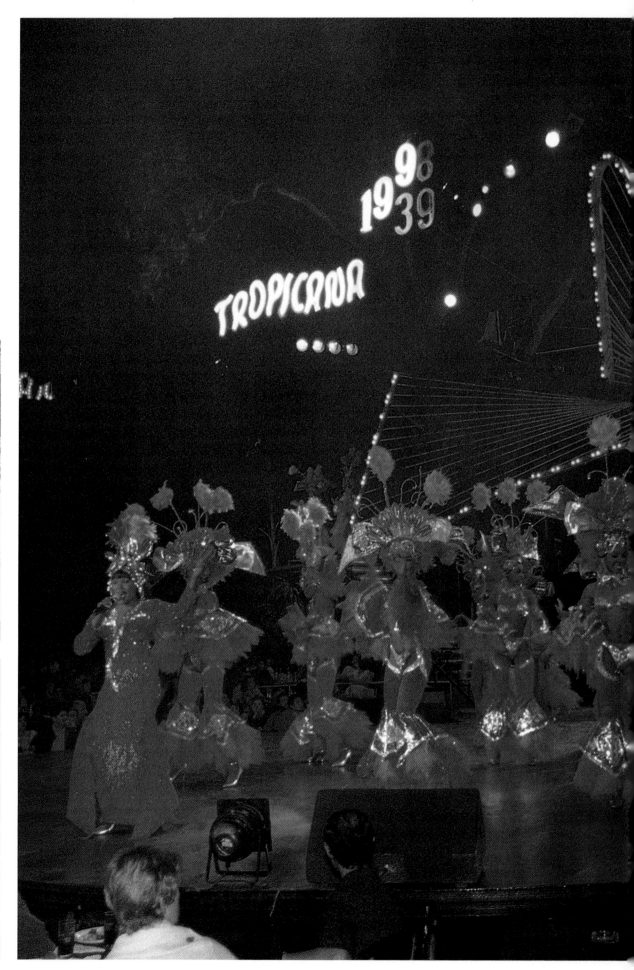

Music, rum and gaiety in the Tropics

110 top *The audience of the Tropicana –
1,400 people every night – sit at tables
arranged on three sides of the stage.
Beautiful showgirls dance and perform
acrobatic numbers, swinging from trapezes
in a whirl of ostrich feathers and sequins,
accompanied by a band of twenty musicians.*

110 bottom *The Tropicana opened its
doors in 1931 and has changed little since
then, except for the roulette and blackjack
tables. Recognized as a valuable source of
income, the floor show has continued to
exist under the Castrist regime.*

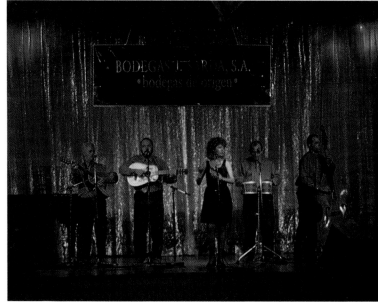

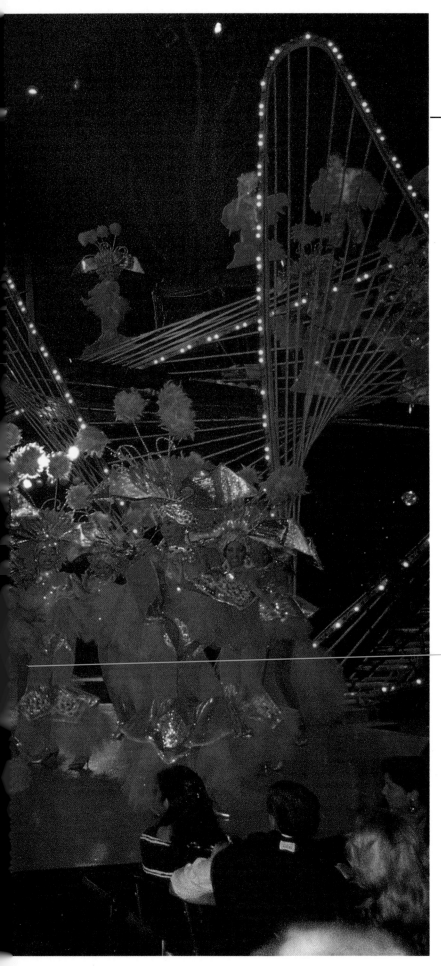

110-111 *Every evening in Havana, the
phantasmagoric show at the Tropicana
gets under way. Much of the
entertainment takes place out-of-doors, in
an amphitheater fringed by a jungle of
tropical trees.*

111 *Bands, singers and variety shows are
the leitmotiv of nightlife in Havana, to
be enjoyed in places like the Café
Havana, depicted in this photo.*

112-113 *Another famous restaurant
in Havana is the Bodeguita del Medio.
Regarding his two favorite cocktails,
Hemingway is supposed to have had a
saying: "My daiquiri in the Floridita, my
mojito in the Bodeguita". Established as
a grocery store in 1942, the Bodeguita del
Medio soon became a bar-cum-
restaurant frequented by writers like
Alejo Carpentier and Nicolàs Guillèn.*

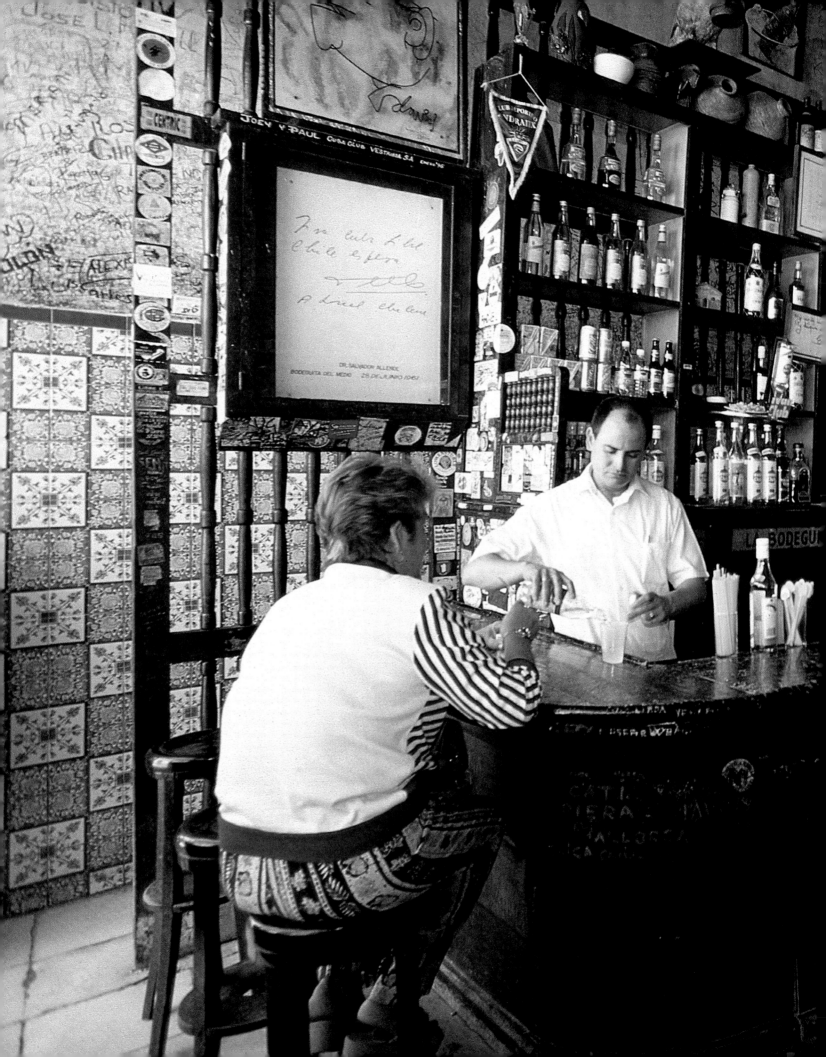

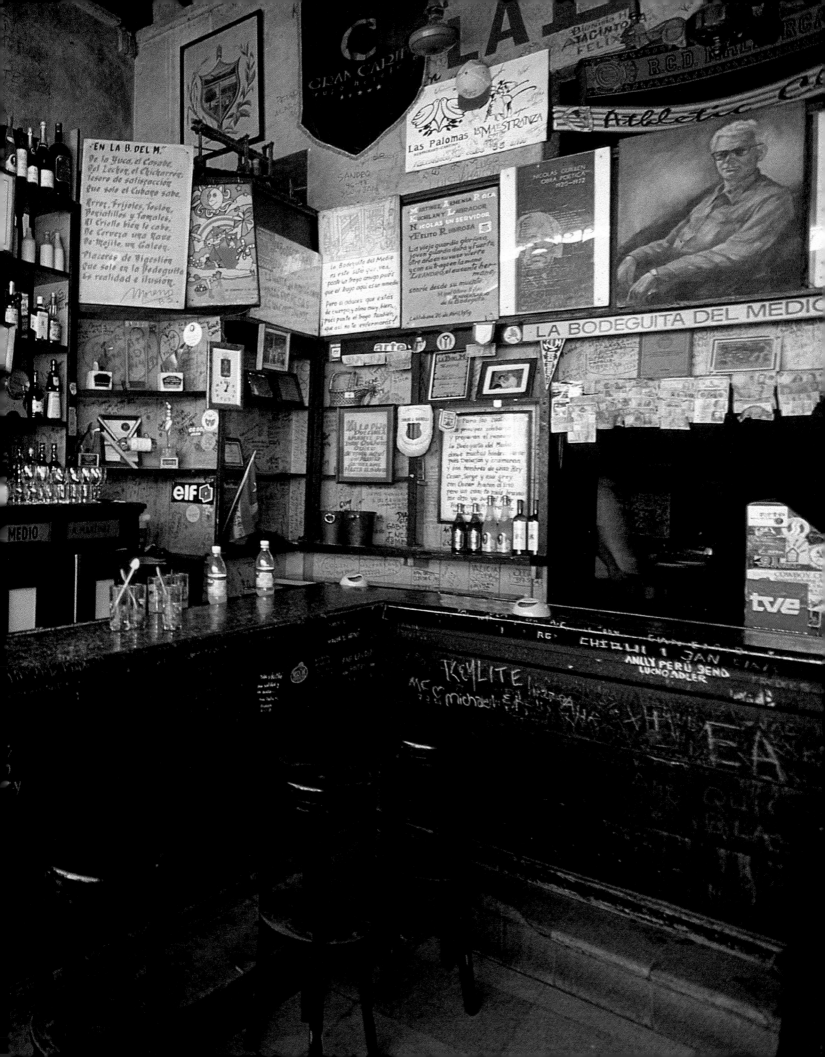

Creative fervor, fantasy and a touch of piety

114 *Cubans are really interested in photography, and they test themselves at every opportunity, using any subject. This street photograph shows a portraitist waiting for potential clients from those that pass by. He is wearing the perfect outfit for the job, complete with a hat to protect from the sun. Using a fan, he seems to find himself perfectly at ease.*

114-115 *Fire-eaters, acrobats, jugglers, souvenir sellers... in the space of just a few years Havana has in many respects started to resemble many other cities across the globe. Gone are the magnificent differences that made it unique in the Western world. The Cuban experiment will nonetheless be remembered as an important lesson by everyone who has visited the island, or who visits it in the future.*

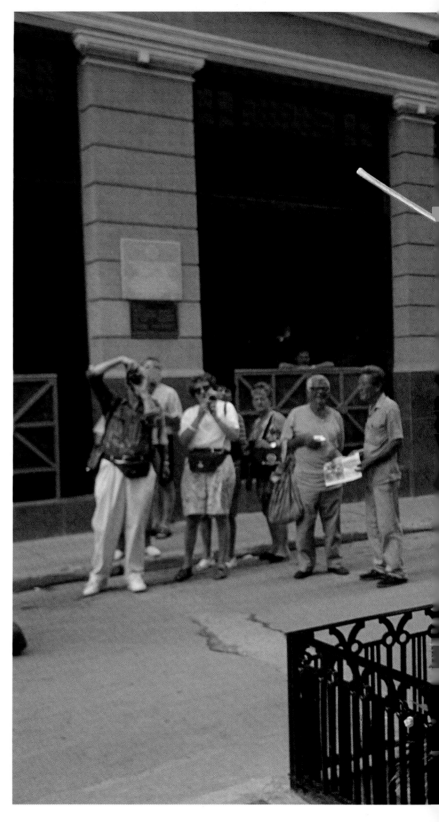

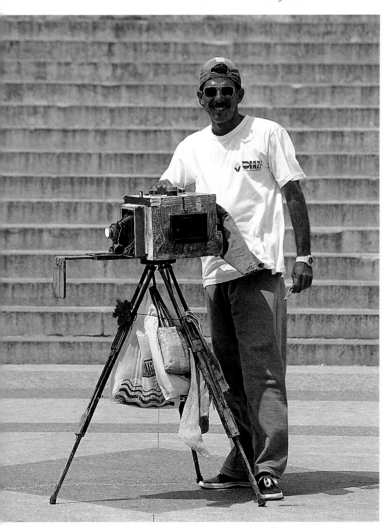

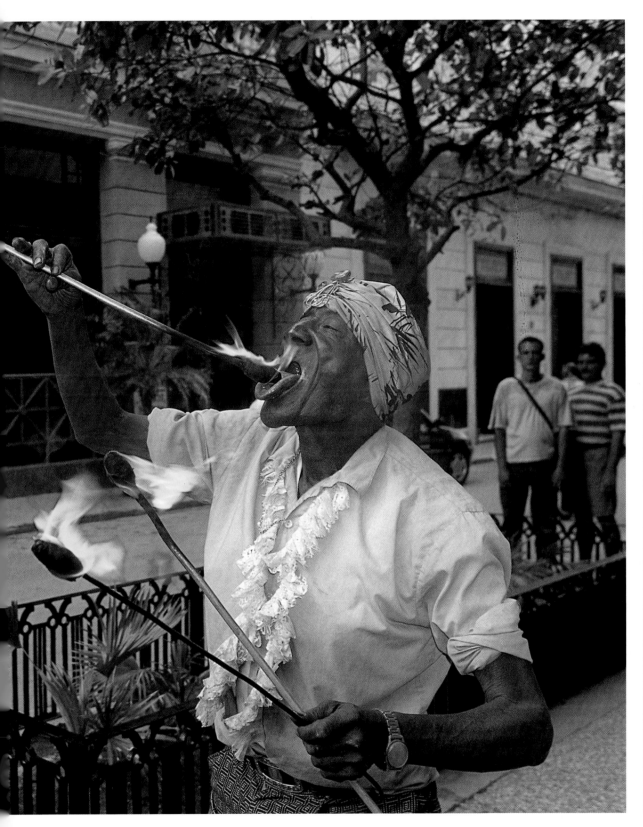

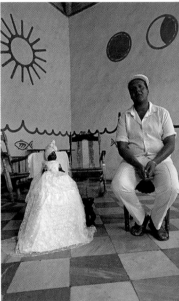

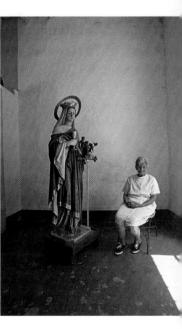

115 top *Alongside the Christian religion, Santería has gained in strength and acquired new followers, called* yoruba, *who dress in plain white. The essence of Santería is its union of Roman Catholicism and traditional African beliefs, necessary in the past to save people who publicly worshipped the* orichas, *African deities, from persecution and accusations of heresy.*

115 bottom *For many years religion was an awkward problem in Cuba. Religious practice was not allowed. But when times began to change, people's dormant beliefs slowly re-surfaced. The Pope's visit to the island naturally played an important role in providing an answer to a difficult situation. In Trinidad this woman smiles contentedly, now that she can live with her statue of the Virgin Mary.*

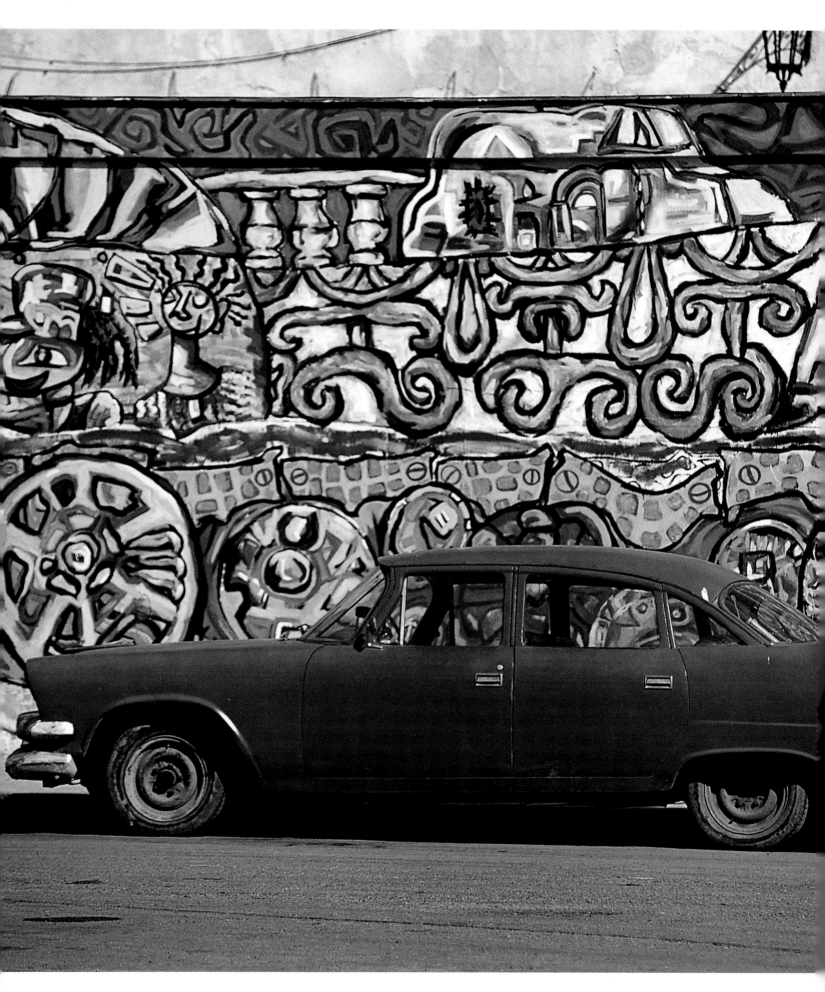

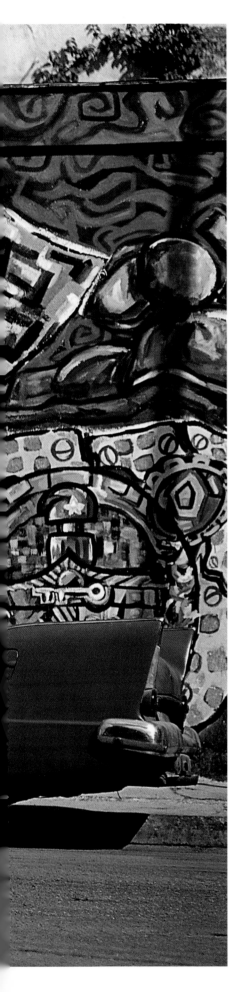

116-117 *Even in the most difficult moments, Cuban flair and imagination have never flagged. This Havana mural, covered with decorative motifs and allegories, is proof. In the foreground, there is an American car from the Fifties, a rather common means of transportation on the Island.*

117 left *The American flag with its stars and stripes has become a demon to be exorcised, by flaunting it as an eye-catching dress. The girl wearing it strolls casually in Plaza de Armas, where books and paintings are on sale in the market established here a few years ago.*

117 top right *Another wall in Calle Jon de Jamel: this one is decorated with bands of red and blue, and broken red and green lines that frame a public phone booth. The eye-catching color*

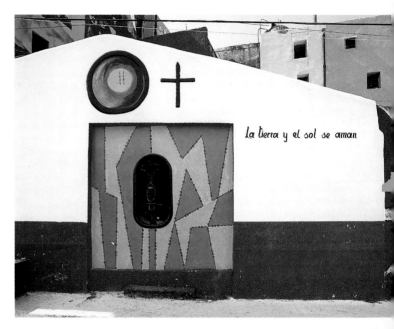

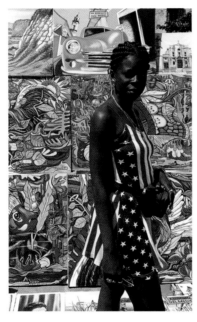

combinations point to clever use of technique and underline young Cubans' aptitude for artistic expression.

117 center right *Calle Jon de Jamel in Havana is like an open-air art gallery where improvising artists have given free rein to their imagination and talent, sometimes with amazing results. The images painted on the walls of houses are an amalgam of iconographic references to Afro-Cuban symbols, comic strips and videogames.*

117 bottom right *Also in Santiago de Cuba artists now sell their work openly in street markets. Their style is often naif: landscapes, animals, portraits of unknown persons or historic figures, all rendered with forceful brushstrokes and bold colors, the very colors of nature in Cuba.*

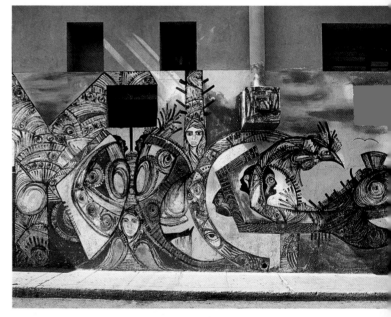

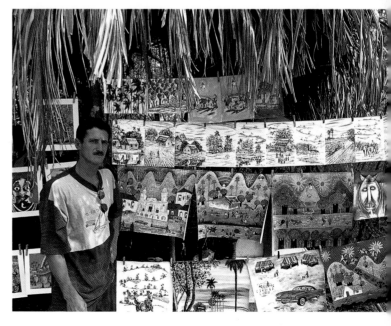

A young country
with a melting-pot legacy

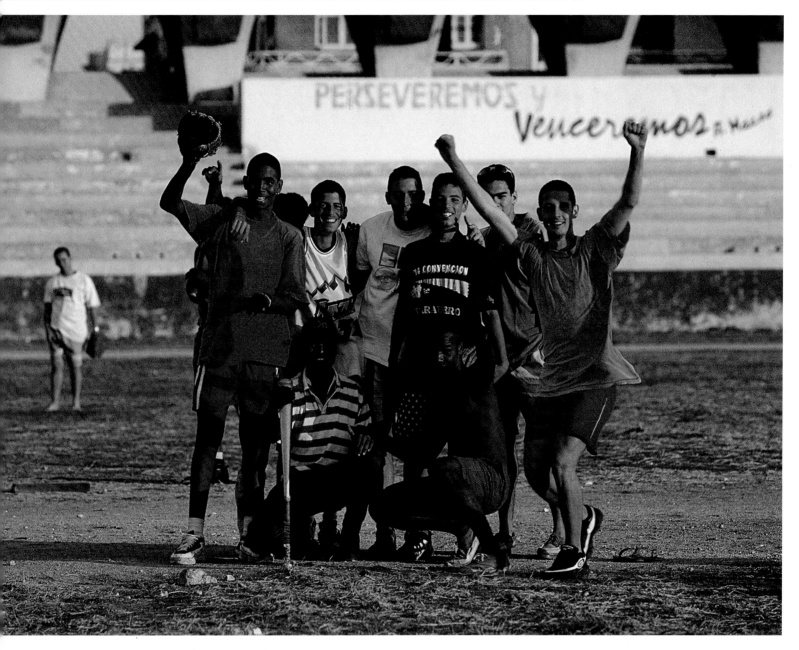

118 *Sports fans, athletes, but above all students: these are the young people of Cuba. They are crazy about sports and follow the undertakings of the greatest champions. They love their island, but they are always updated on what is happening in the rest of the world. Similarly, they listen to popular music but prefer rock n'roll and, in particular, jazz, modified according to the tendencies and tastes typical of a Caribbean island.*

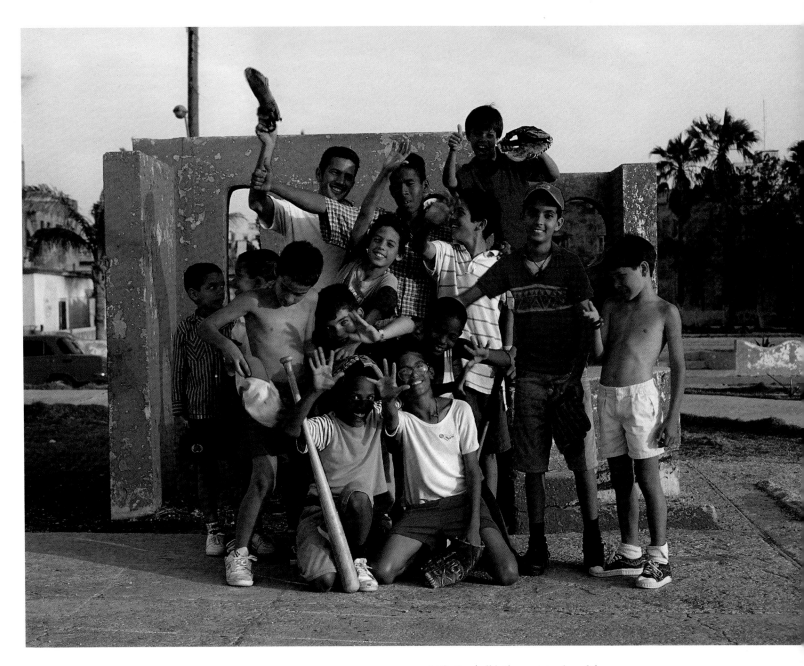

119 *Baseball is the great passion of the younger boys. Prominent in all the island's sports stadiums are posters with Fidel Castro's slogan: "Sport is the people's right". Every year almost 100,000 elementary schoolchildren take part in athletics competitions organized as part of inter-school tournaments. The best are invited to apply for admission to high schools for youngsters with outstanding athletic potential.*

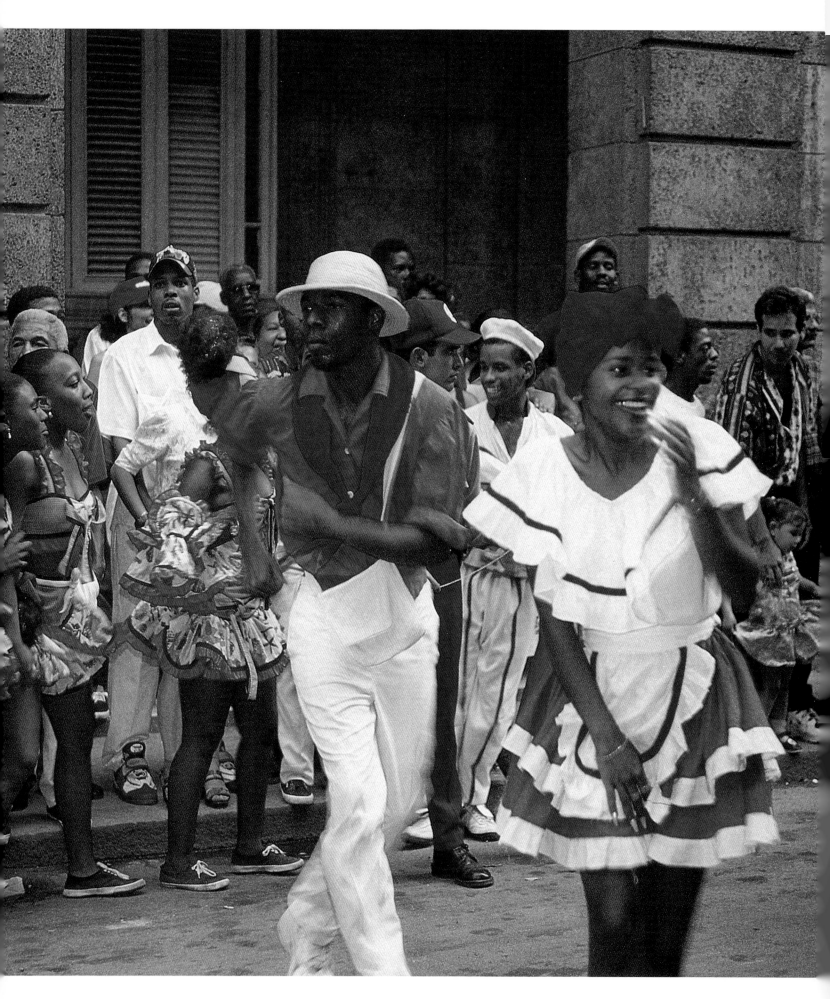

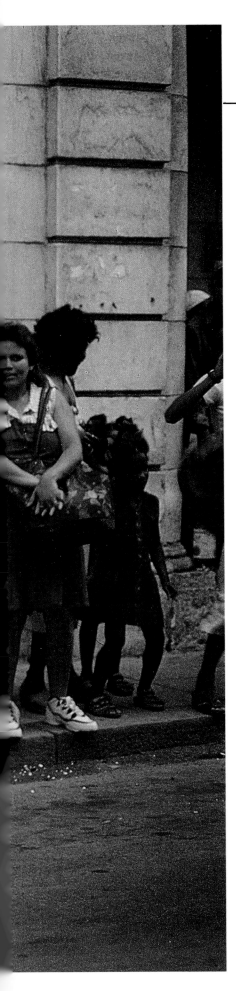

It's carnival time, again!

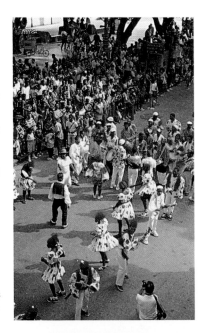

120-121 *Havana's parade of floats and figures in carnival costumes is known as the* desfile: *it takes place every year in the second half of July and last 10 days – and 10 nights too, when celebrations are perhaps even more exuberant.*

121 left *Pavements and balconies of houses overlooking the Malecón are soon packed with families wishing to join in these long-awaited festivities. Havana's Carnival is truly spectacular but it attracts fewer crowds than the one held in Santiago de Cuba, which spreads to every corner of town.*

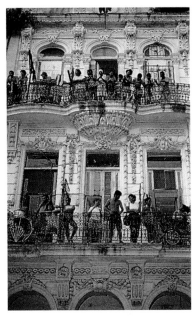

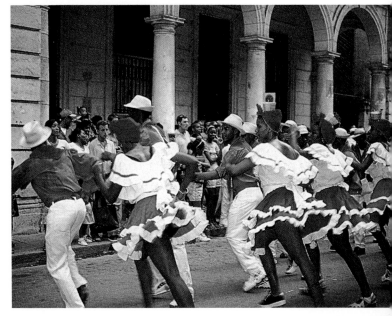

121 right *Groups of paraders dance nonstop with boundless energy and enthusiasm, and the spectators also get caught up in the frenzy and fun. Late into the night the festivities continue in the city's clubs and bars. The procession of floats moves off in the late afternoon and parades along the Malecón – obviously closed to traffic – passing in front of the Riviera and Nacional hotels, first in one direction, then in the other. Stands for spectators are set up along the route, together with makeshift eating places, bars, places to dance and, above all, beer vendors.*

122-123 *The loud colors and flamboyant designs of the costumes – as well as the dance routines and the catchy new rhythms played by the bands on the floats – are an important part of the spectacle and often contribute much to the overall success of the event .*

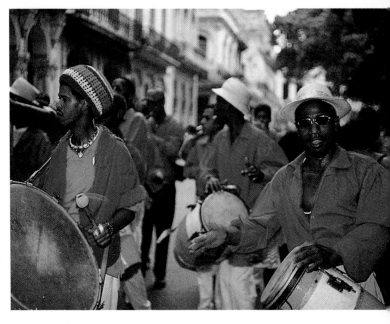

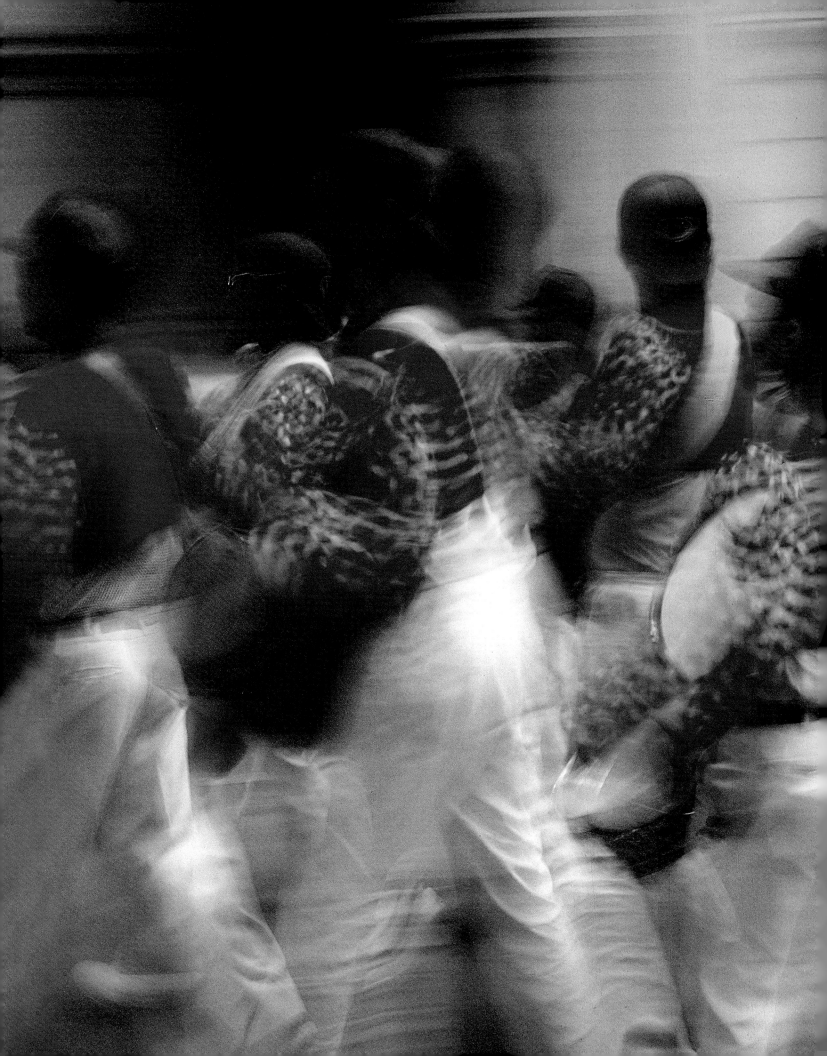

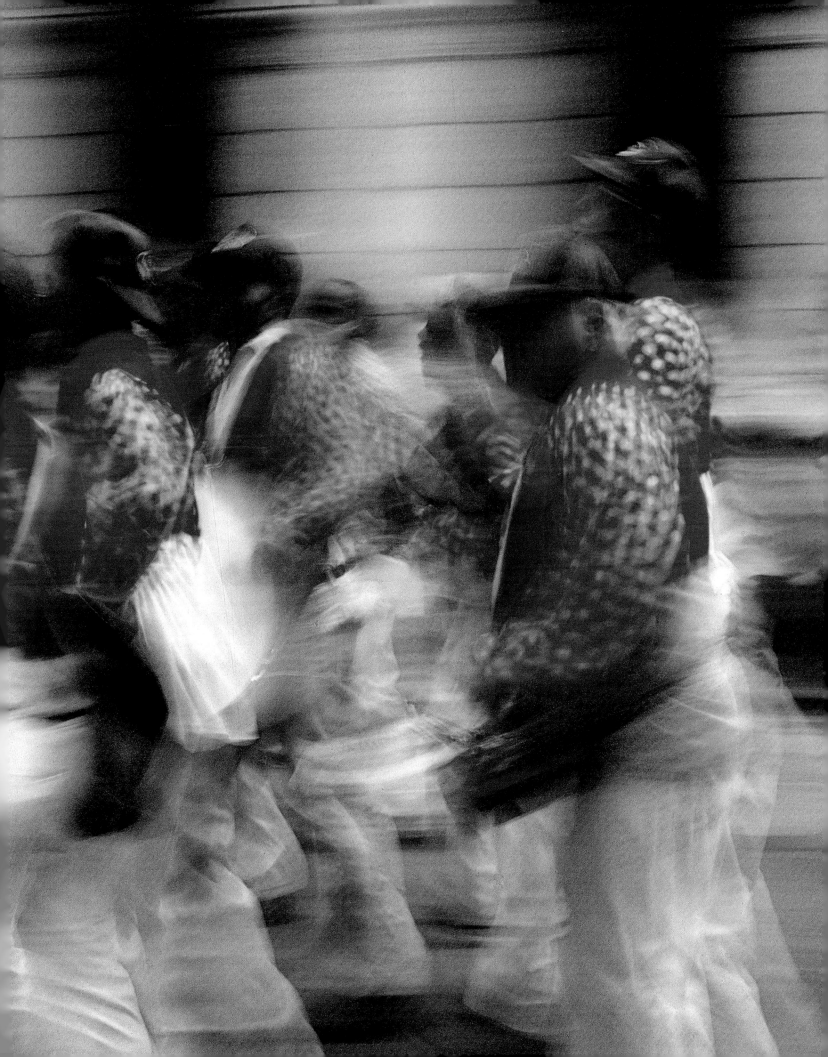

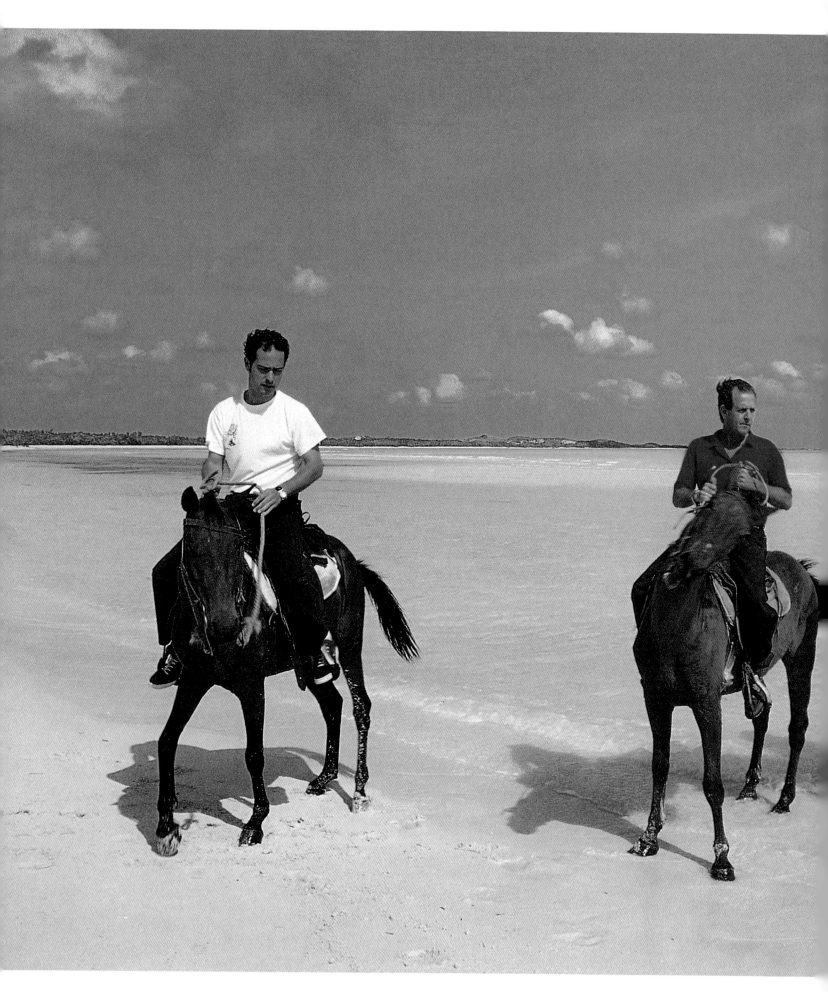

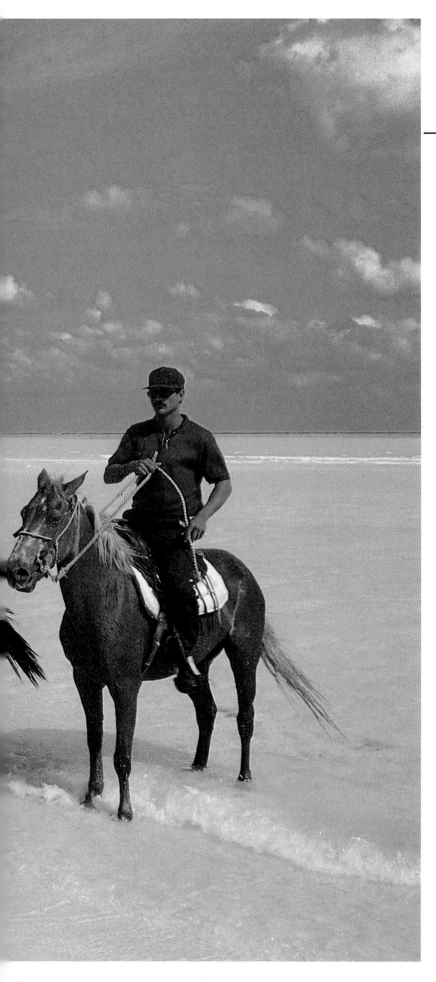

A paradise of sun, sea and sand

124-125 *In Cuba you can go horseback-riding along the shore. The beaches are fine white sand, dazzling in the reflected light of the sun shining in an almost always cloudless sky. Horses can be hired everywhere and no equestrian skills are needed to ride at a gentle trot on the loveliest beaches in the world.*

125 *Two sunbathers relax at the water's edge. The waves caress their bodies while the sun's rays tan their skin. "Tomar el sol", they say in Cuba; sunbathing is*

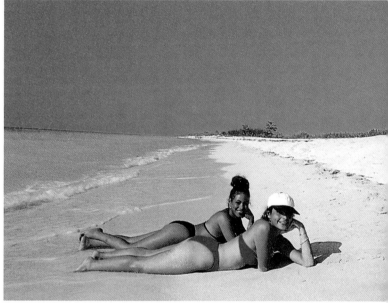

certainly an enjoyable way to pass the time. And no effort is needed either.

126-127 *A more tiring but certainly more adventurous pastime is windsurfing. A gently undulated but not choppy sea, constant breezes, an agreeable water temperature and hot sun: the perfect ingredients to satisfy vacationers who take to the ocean on a sailboard.*

128 *An American car from the '50s is no rarity in Cuba. The revolution made them a permanent part of the urban landscape and thousands are still seen on the island's roads: many are in working order while others have succumbed to engine troubles. But their bodywork, polished with loving care, can be a stunning sight. Often these old cars are used for weddings.*

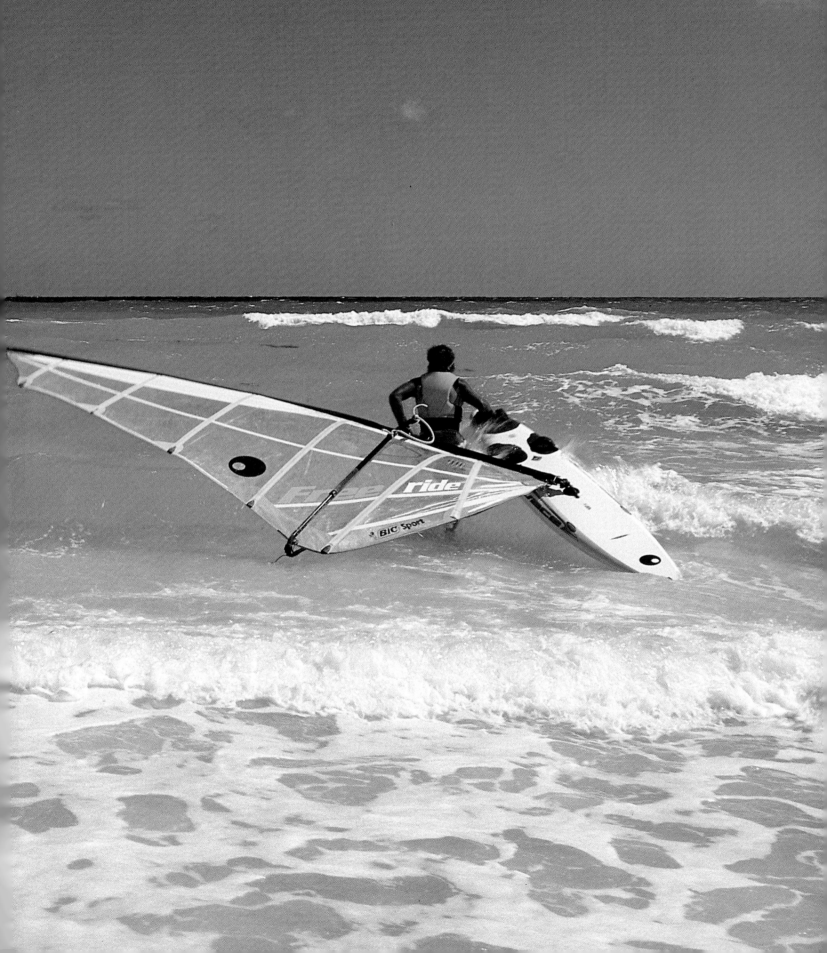

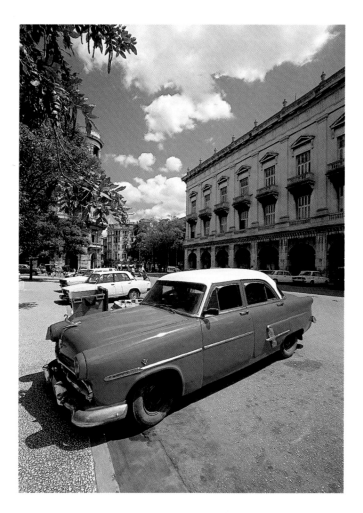

All the pictures are by Antonio Attini / Archivio White Star except:

Livio Bourbon/Archivio White Star: pages 116-117.

Map by Cristina Franco